MW00882454

Note for Librarians: a cataloguing record for this book that includes Dewey Decimal Classification and US Library of Congress numbers is available from the Library and Archives of Canada. The complete cataloguing record can be obtained from their online database at:
www.collectionscanada.ca/amicus/index-e.html
ISBN 1-4120-4456-1

Scripture taken from the NEW AMERICAN STANDARD BIBLE®
© Copyright 1960, 1962, 1963, 1968, 1971, 1973, 1975, 1977
by The Lockman Foundation
Used by permission. (www.lockman.org)

Author Photo by Olan Mills Portrait Studio

TRAFFORD

Offices in Canada, USA, Ireland, UK and Spain
This book was published *on-demand* in cooperation with Trafford Publishing. On-demand publishing is a unique process and service of making a book available for retail sale to the public taking advantage of on-demand manufacturing and Internet marketing. On-demand publishing includes promotions, retail sales, manufacturing, order fulfilment, accounting and collecting royalties on behalf of the author.
Book sales for North America and international:
Trafford Publishing, 6E–2333 Government St.,
Victoria, BC v8T 4P4 CANADA
phone 250 383 6864 (toll-free 1 888 232 4444)
fax 250 383 6804; email to orders@trafford.com
Book sales in Europe:
Trafford Publishing (UK) Ltd., Enterprise House, Wistaston Road Business Centre,
Wistaston Road, Crewe, Cheshire CW2 7RP UNITED KINGDOM
phone 01270 251 396 (local rate 0845 230 9601)
facsimile 01270 254 983; orders.uk@trafford.com
Order online at:
trafford.com/04-2264

10 9 8 7 6 5 4 3

ACKNOWLEGMENTS

I would like to thank all of those who were committed to pray with me in this endeavor. Thank you for your faithfulness in lifting me up and in encouraging me. Should the Father choose to use this to minister to anyone, you have co-labored in the lives of those individuals with me. Thank you, Sarah, Madeline, Lucibeth and Emma Kate, Ann and Ann, Sara and Chris, Brenda, Michelle, Tricia and Kirby.

I also owe a huge debt of gratitude to the Monday night BIO ladies who have listened and given feedback on all of the materials presented in this book. My thanks to each one of you.

Thank you, Cheryl, for your professional editing. But more importantly, thank you for years of faithful friendship.

Thank you, Chris Cartledge (Promark, Inc.) for coming to the rescue with graphic help. Without your work no one would be able to see the Fork images in the text. Thanks also for the wonderful cover design.

Thanks to Jim B. for resurrecting Chapter 4 from the cyber graveyard. You are brilliant! Thank you, Ernie, for your help with the final formatting. You rescued the clueless.

Thank you, Dr. Keller, for your faithful proclamation of the Word at Redeemer Presbyterian. You mentor me through your tape ministry, constantly pointing me back to Jesus and reminding me of "right side living."

Finally, I would like to thank my husband, Ron, for traveling the continuing spiritual journey of growth in grace with me. Thank you for being my sounding board, my wise counsel and my best friend.

DEDICATION

This book is dedicated to my Savior, the One who delights in redeeming what is lost and in using the weak, the foolish and the things that are not so that any boasting might be in Him.

CONTENTS

THE GOSPEL FOR THE VISUAL LEARNER:
The Fork Illustration

INTRODUCTION

My husband and I have three sons. Our middle son was diagnosed with autism when he was two years old. Many autistic individuals are visual learners who not only comprehend information more effectively when it is presented visually, but they actually think in pictures. Over the past decade, the Lord has used our son's learning style to develop visual teaching skills within us.

This book is an attempt to provide those who learn visually with a presentation of how we grow and change as believers. As I began seeking ways to communicate the truth of the gospel message using imagery, the Lord gave me what I call "The Fork Illustration."

It has been my privilege to share this visual representation with women's groups and youth. I stand back and watch as the Holy Spirit uses a diagram to drive home the message of the freedom that we have in Christ. He applies the message of how real and lasting change takes place in the life of a believer through the use of this concrete image.

Even those who are not "visual" learners can benefit from exposure to this illustration. Engaging more of our senses in learning specific concepts increases our ability to comprehend and retain information. When we not only read about the gospel or hear the message of life in Christ taught, but are able to see a framework upon which we can hang our life experience of it, it becomes more readily applicable and has a greater impact on daily living.

It is my prayer, as you examine this material, that the Lord would use it to make the gospel more vivid and meaningful to you on a moment-by-moment basis in your life.

Leslie C. Hughes

6

Preface

The gospel of grace is a message for everyone. Both those who are believers and those who are not need the liberation from sin that Jesus Christ provides.

The Fork Illustration's visual representation of the gospel is necessary for the non-believer who must "see" the message for the first time. The non-Christian needs to experience the *initial* movement from the domain of darkness to the kingdom of light. He needs understanding and enlightenment from the Spirit of God as to the nature of man and the redemption provided by God in Christ.

The Fork's graphic depiction of the gospel is vital for the Christian who needs to experience the *recurring* movement from life in the flesh to abiding in Christ. Perhaps you are a Christian who has picked up this book and your thoughts are traveling along these lines: "I can see how the gospel is essential for non-Christians, but I have heard the gospel. In fact, I have a good grasp on how to communicate the essential elements of its message to others. Even if I am a visual learner, I don't need a book for the auditorially challenged learner to teach me something that I already know." But the gospel is also essential for believers. It is relevant and pertinent for *all* of the Christian life, not just initiation into it.

If your initial reaction is similar to that described above, you probably have a good understanding of the gospel's past functioning in your life. You understand that you were saved by faith and can look back to a particular day, or even specific time, in your life when you received forgiveness and righteousness based on the finished work of Christ on your behalf. Or maybe you are one of those Christians who can't remember a day in your life when you did not know about Christ and His loving sacrifice on your behalf. Perhaps, in addition, you even have an inkling of the gospel's future purpose in your life. You realize that one day you will be called to stand before the King of the universe and give an accounting. Obviously, the reason He will let you into His heaven is because the blood of Jesus has cleansed you from sin and given you a right standing before Him. But if you believe that the gospel is primarily for the unbeliever, may I suggest that you are deficient in your knowledge of the current and ongoing application of the grace of God in your life.

The Fork Illustration is a depiction not only of how we gain entrance into a life of grace, but also how we are called to appropriate grace continually. In every moment of our lives, we are living in one of the three positions represented on the Fork. Understanding what these positions are and how movement is made from any one to another is vital for remaining in the desired location.

I was recently asked to share the Fork Illustration at a Ski Conference for a senior high youth group. The youth director, being a clever and creative guy, came up with the theme for the weekend, "Gospel Dinnerware." All of the teens were curious as to what a "fork" had to do with the Christian life. While most arrived knowing that the gospel of grace was the message that had saved them, many left with an increased awareness of how the gospel was essential and relevant to life every minute of every day. Being able to identify the three alternatives and evaluate where they were functionally living at any given moment was revolutionary in their walks with Christ.

If you are a non-believer who is unsure of your convictions about Christianity, I encourage you to read on and see if you can locate yourself on the Fork. Perhaps you have viewed Christianity as something far different from what Scripture claims that it is.

If you are a Christian, I urge you to press on and seek to evaluate your functional living in light of the three possible options. It could be that you are self-sufficiently living like an adult who needs no help, or perhaps even like an openly rebellious child. If so as you read, ask the Spirit to remind you of your position as a beloved child of the Father.

Chapter 1
The Fork Illustration

We often hear pastors and teachers tell us that the Christian life is a "balance." Unfortunately, when many hear this they tend to think that a godly life is a happy medium between legalism and licentiousness which can be diagramed as follows:

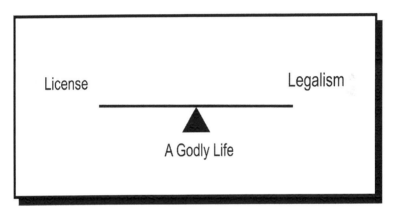

Those who have been raised with some form of religious influence intuitively know that a life of licentiousness, that is a life of open rebellion or total disregard for the law of God, is wrong. In addition we read this concerning those not reared with religious traditions, "For when Gentiles who do not have the Law do instinctively the things of the Law, these, not having the Law, are a law to themselves, in that they show the work of the Law written in their hearts, their consciences bearing witness, and their thoughts alternately accusing or else defending them..." (Romans 2:14,15). Here the apostle Paul states that even those who are untutored in spiritual things have some innate sense of the moral vacancy of lawlessness. Likewise, we also know that a life of legalism, a life focused on law and rule keeping, is also wrong. This is evidenced by the numerous times in the gospel accounts where Jesus is seen openly rebuking the Pharisees, the religious teachers of the day, for their unhealthy obsession with the law. An example is found in Matthew 23 where Jesus pronounces seven "woes" against these hypocritical teachers. So, if a life of law breaking is wrong and a life of law keeping for righteousness is wrong, many rationalize that a properly lived Christian life that is pleasing to God is somewhere between legalism and license. They conclude that the Christian life is a balance.

But what many fail to recognize is that Scripture tells us that legalism and license are two aspects of our flesh and that both are opposed to life as a true believer. Each is a representation of a life lived in the flesh apart from God, and both are in contrast with a life lived by the Spirit.

If that is true, where then do we draw the authentic Christian life on the above diagram? What needs to be understood is that the Christian life is not even on the continuum drawn above at all! Take your finger and place it on the words, "GODLY LIFE" at the center of the line. Now, lift your finger straight off of the page about five inches. This is where the real Christian life is in relation to the diagram before you. You see, the continuum drawn on the page represents life in the Flesh. The Christian life is a totally different *dimension* from this. It is a life not based on law, whether breaking the law or keeping the law, but it is a life based on relationship. It is a life of grace and freedom. So how can we draw this in a two dimensional form so that we can further explore the contrasts between the two? We sketch out the Fork Illustration this way:

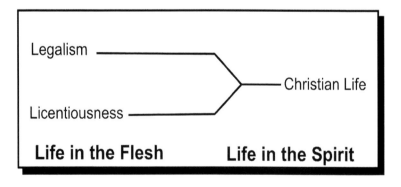

Let's look at this in detail. Life on the left side of the Fork is life in the flesh. All behaviors on the left side of the Fork are driven by **fear, pride and unbelief**. Life on the right side of the Fork is life in the Spirit. All behaviors produced on the right side of the Fork are driven by **freedom, humility and faith**.

DESIRES OF THE FLESH and LIFE UNDER LAW

In Galatians 5 the Apostle Paul is contrasting life in the flesh with life in the Spirit. In verse 16 he says, "But I say to you, 'Walk by the Spirit and you will not carry out the desires of the flesh.'" And then in verse 18 he says, "But if you are led by the Spirit, you are not under law." As we look at these two verses, it can be clearly seen on the fork that Paul is contrasting these two different aspects of our flesh with life in the Spirit. The Apostle Paul lists several examples of rebellious living in verses 19-21: "...immorality, impurity, sensuality, idolatry, sorcery, enmities, strife, jealousy, outbursts of anger, disputes, dissensions, factions, envying, drunkenness, carousing, and things like these...." This is just a partial list of the deeds which are evidence of licentious living. This law breaking is what readily comes to mind as we consider what constitutes ungodly living. But what Paul is demonstrating here through Galatians 5:16 *and* 18 is that it is equally ungodly to "live under the law." This is life on the top left hand side of the Fork, the life of law keeping unto righteousness.

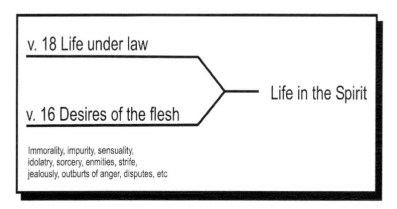

v. 18 Life under law

Life in the Spirit

v. 16 Desires of the flesh

Immorality, impurity, sensuality,
idolatry, sorcery, enmities, strife,
jealously, outburts of anger, disputes, etc

What does Paul mean by "life under the law?" To live under the law means to keep the law as a means of obtaining or maintaining a righteousness that one can present to God so that He would be required to accept the bearer. In his book entitled, *The Cross Centered Life*, C. J. Mahaney defines legalism this way: "Legalism is seeking to achieve forgiveness from God and acceptance by God through obedience to God." He goes on to say, "Legalism claims that the death of Jesus on the cross was either unnecessary or insufficient. It essentially says to God, 'Your plan didn't work. The cross wasn't enough and I need to add my good works to it to be saved.'"[1]

DOMAIN OF DARKNESS and KINGDOM OF LIGHT

In Colossians 1:13 Paul says, "For He has delivered us from the domain of darkness and transferred us to the Kingdom of His beloved Son." The left side of the Fork Illustration represents the "domain of darkness." The right side of the Fork denotes the Kingdom of Light. For someone to have been transferred to the right side of the Fork, Paul says that they have been delivered there by Christ. This deliverance occurs through justification.

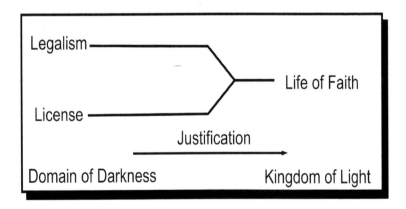

Justification is a one-time event in which God legally declares an individual to be righteous. Again, in an attempt to use more concrete methods to teach abstract concepts, the four math operations can be used as a tool to aid in remembering and teaching the essential characteristics of justification. The four math operations are addition, subtraction, multiplication and division. First, in justification something is *subtracted* (-). Our sin is taken away, or forgiven. Also, when a person is justified, something is *added* (+). We are given Christ's perfect record. It is credited to our account and when the Father looks at us, He sees only Christ's perfectly lived life. We are legally given Christ's righteousness. Thirdly, the math operation of multiplication helps us remember that justification is a one-time (X) event. It happens at a specific point in time and never needs repetition. While it is different from sanctification, it is related in that justification is the basis for sanctification. Sanctification is an on-going process through which a believer grows up *actually* into what he or she has already *legally* been declared to be (i.e., righteous). Sanctification flows out of justification. In his book, *The Church*, Edmond Clowney says this of the relation between justification and sanctification: "Classical Reformed theology distinguishes between God's **act** of justification (and adoption) and His continuing **work** of sanctification."[2] An act is an isolated incident as opposed to a work, which is a sustained process. And, finally, the operation of division (or more specifically, the words, "divided **by**") is to remind us that justification is **by** (/) grace through faith.

Now, let me take just a moment and share a personal illustration to emphasize a point. While we can use these math operations to remember the essential components of justification, we need to keep in mind that justification presupposes the fallen condition of man. This was brought home to me as I shared these four components with a non-Christian friend of mine. Sherry and I had been running together routinely for months. She was a practicing Catholic, but I doubted that she had a full understanding of the gospel message. The gospel message tells us that we are totally sinful, yet infinitely loved. While I did not doubt that she believed she was a sinner due to the teaching that she had received in her religious background, I did not think that she had ever heard, with the "ears of her heart," that grace was available for sinners. She listened intently as I explained, between the huffing and puffing, these four basic aspects of justification. After hearing, she asked some pointed questions about when and how this could happen to her. Then she made an insightful observation that I will not forget. She said to me, "You know, this concept assumes that I have a sin problem." While Sherry did not doubt her fallen condition, it was a great reminder to me that justification is the solution to a problem which many would not even recognize, let alone acknowledge.

So, the non-believer lives positionally on the left side of the Fork. If you are a non-believer desiring a personal relationship with God and a guarantee of eternity in His presence, an initial positional movement from the left side of the Fork to the right is required. This movement is only achieved through an acknowledgment of and repentance from sin, and through faith in Jesus Christ alone for forgiveness and righteousness before God. Sin, seen both in law breaking and in law keeping for righteousness, must be recognized, confessed and forsaken. Christ alone must be trusted as the basis for acceptance and approval before God. The initial rightward movement is only possible as God extends grace and faith to you from which you are enabled to respond in belief to the message of reconciliation. Nothing else is required, and, in fact, attempts to bring anything besides "nothing" demonstrates a complete lack of understanding of the transferring inertia of the gospel message.

Justified believers live positionally on the right side of the Fork, but unfortunately choose to spend much of life functionally operating on the left. As we get into Chapter 4, we will explore this in greater detail.

OBVIOUS FACE and SNEAKY FACE

Licentious living is the *obvious* face that our flesh wears. For example, we would never go out and have an extra-marital affair and assume that we could use it to recommend us or make us acceptable to God. We would never come from a clandestine sexual rendezvous and then in our hearts say to God, "I've just committed adultery, now You owe me! Now, You'll bless me!" It's obvious to even the most hardened heart that there is a problem with this picture. But legalism is the *sneaky* face of our flesh. The sneaky face of our flesh uses outward conformity to the law to recommend us to God. We spend time at a Bible study fellowship meeting and then in our hearts we experience the subtle feeling that wants to say to God, "I've just studied your Word, now You owe me! Now, You'll bless me." In licentiousness we are living *from* God, but in legalism we are living *for* God. Neither is authentic Christianity. True Christianity is living *in* God.

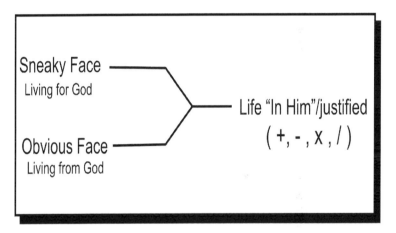

Sneaky Face
Living for God

Obvious Face
Living from God

Life "In Him"/justified
$(+ , - , X , /)$

The problem with both the sneaky face of the flesh and the obvious face of the flesh is that in neither position is one mindful of one's justification. Neither is resting in Christ's righteousness alone on one's behalf for salvation. Life in God is a life of abiding. It is the life Jesus speaks of in John 15 when He states that He is the vine and we are the branches. He calls us to abide in Him and in His love.

REBELLION and REFORMATION

Another way of explaining life on the left is that a life of license is a life of *moral rebellion;* it is a life of *indulging the flesh.* The corresponding life of legalism is a life of *moral reformation;* it is a life of *restraining the flesh.* Moral reformation is our attempting to use the law to change us.

This is not the purpose of the law, nor has it ever been God's intent for the law. Many have used the illustration of an x-ray to explain the law. If a person has a broken bone, the law is like an x-ray. It can reveal that there is a problem, and even specifically pin-point the location of the problem, but the law cannot fix the problem. Just like an x-ray cannot repair a broken bone, neither does the law have the power to rectify the sin problem within us.

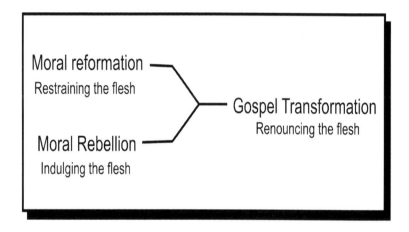

In contrast to this, on the right side of the Fork Illustration we find *gospel transformation*, a life of *renouncing the flesh*. What do I mean by gospel transformation and renouncing the flesh? Gospel transformation is a phrase that summarizes the idea of allowing the truth of the gospel message to captivate us at a heart level. To the degree we are able to grasp the depth of our depravity and the vastness of God's love for us, we are proportionately transformed into the image of Christ. Both of the aspects of our flesh depicted on the left side of the Fork are renounced. We declare an unconditional surrender of our lives and acknowledge Christ's sufficient sacrifice as our only means and hope for salvation.

Life on the left side of the Fork is life independent from God. It is an autonomous life. A licentious heart says, *"I want to be my own Master or Lord."* It says, "No one can tell me how to live. I know what is best for me. I will run my own life based on what feels or seems right to me." A legalistic heart says, *"I want to be my own Savior."* It says, "I can be good enough to save myself. My sins are not so significant that I can't work to pay them off on my own. I don't need anyone or anything. I am independent and can make it on my own." How many times have you said or heard someone say, "Yes, she's accepted Christ as her Savior and Lord?" Do you realize what that phrase, "to accept Jesus as Savior and Lord," really means? Can you see concretely, on the Fork, how it is a renunciation of the flesh in its entirety? To accept Jesus as Savior and Lord is to renounce the flesh, in *both* of its aspects.

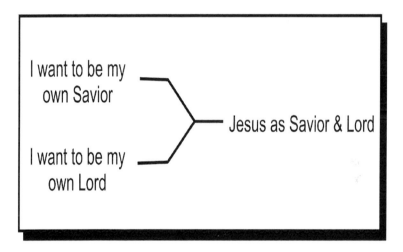

Gospel transformation stands in direct contrast with moral rebellion *and* moral reformation. Gospel transformation focuses on internal change. It is a radical, heart level change that will have enduring results. Moral reformation is concerned with external change and is produced by law keeping. While it may appear to have benefits in the short run, moral reformation does not deal with the heart, and any observable differences in the life are destined to be short lived. As Christians, we desire to be transformed into the image of Christ (2 Corinthians 3:18). This can only occur as the Spirit of God works within the heart of a believer and produces expressions of the life of Christ that is within.

Let's continue to develop the Fork as we look at other ways of explaining the concepts represented. Licentiousness says, "*I do something for me.*" Legalism says, "*I do something for God.*" Yet, life on the right side of the Fork, life as a child of God, as one who is living out of his or her identity "in Christ" says, "*God does something for me.*" God provides forgiveness and gives a righteousness to me so that He can accept me.

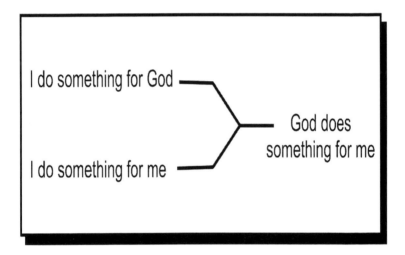

I do something for God

I do something for me

God does something for me

Licentiousness is a life lived *disregarding the law*, while legalism is a life lived *doing the law*. In contrast to this, Paul tells us in Romans 10:4, "For Christ is the end of the law for righteousness to everyone who believes." This means that Christianity is about *dying to the law* for righteousness. I love this verse and can always remember it because of Citizen's Band radio. Are you old enough to remember back in the 1970's when CB radios were a popular fad? In Citizen's Band lingo, a 10:4 was an affirmative answer. Eighteen wheeler truck drivers were frequently heard chanting, "That's a big 10:4, good buddy!" Well, that is how I remember Romans 10:4. The fact that

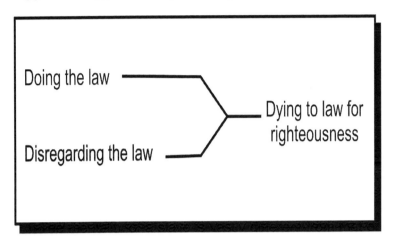

Christ is the end of the law for righteousness for me is the biggest "10:4, good buddy!" that my heart has ever heard!

Doing the law ——————

Disregarding the law ——————

Dying to law for righteousness

ORPHAN and SLAVE or SON and FREE

Life on the left side of the Fork is life as an *orphan*. It is a life of *slavery and bondage*. In contrast, life on the right side of the Fork, a life lived out of our identity in Christ, is life as a *son or daughter* of the King and is a life of *freedom and liberty*.

The mentality of a slave is vastly different from that of a son. A slave lives in fear, while a son lives securely. A slave obeys the commands of a master in order to secure his position within a household. A son obeys the rules of a father because he knows that his position within the household is already secure.

An orphan is alone and must be self-sufficient. By definition, he is independent and has no one to ensure that he receives even essentials for life. He must secure all necessities and possessions by his own strength. An orphan's life is filled with anxiety over meeting future needs. In contrast, a son is in relationship with his father. His father provides all things fundamental for life and growth. The son is dependent on the generosity and resources of the father for all basic needs. His heart is at rest as he trusts the father to provide all that is required.

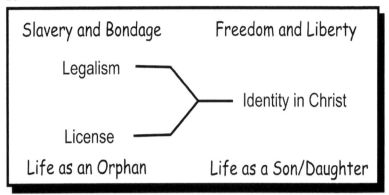

Life on the left side of the Fork is all about what you *do*. It focuses on how you **act**. In opposition to this, life on the right side of the Fork is all about what you *believe.* It is all about who you **are**.

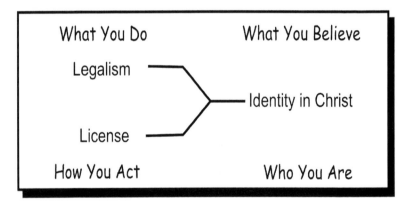

In this chapter I have introduced the Fork Illustration and its components. Teaching by contrast is a powerful means of instruction. Jesus often used contrast to emphasize specific truths He wished to communicate. I have attempted to teach in a visual format what the gospel message is, by showing what it is not. Let's continue and put some Scriptural references on the Fork Illustration to see how often the concepts are presented to us in the Word of God.

Chapter 2
Seeing Scripture on the Fork

Now that you've been exposed to the framework of the Fork Illustration, let's look at some passages of Scripture that are probably familiar to you and see how the Fork explains the teachings they present. I have already mentioned Galatians 5, so let's begin there.

Galatians 5:6

The apostle Paul wrote the book of Galatians. In it, Paul is more assertive and forceful than in any of his other epistles. Paul is concerned for the churches in the region of Galatia because a group of teachers called "Judaizers" have come in to the churches and are presenting a false message to the new converts there. These false teachers are claiming that strict adherence to Old Testament law - in particular, mandates concerning circumcision - is necessary for salvation. In essence, they are teaching that something must be added to faith in order for salvation to be effective. Paul strongly argues against this throughout this letter and urges the Galatian believers to remember that they were saved by grace through faith alone, and that this is the way they are to continue in their Christian lives. The theme of the book is that not only is our justification by faith alone, but so, too, is our sanctification. In Galatians 5:6, Paul tells them, "For in Christ Jesus neither circumcision nor uncircumcision means anything, but faith working through love." What Paul is saying can be represented on the Fork as follows:

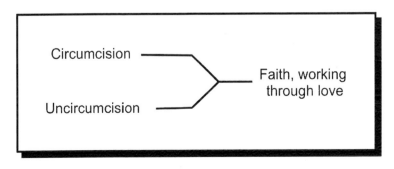

You see, Paul uses "uncircumcision" to represent license, life apart from law, law breaking. He cites circumcision as law keeping for righteousness, or legalism. Paul is reminding the Galatians that what is important is faith. He emphasizes that *neither* circumcision nor uncircumcision is of any value. No deeds produced by motivations on the left side of the Fork ever are. All of these behaviors flow out of fear, pride and a lack of belief in the truth of the Word of God. Works of righteousness and acts of love that flow out of a belief in the message of the gospel are what he calls "faith working through love." These acts of righteousness are motivated by faith, freedom and humility, as are all behaviors on the right side of the Fork. If the Galatian believers understood the message that they are deeply sinful yet dearly loved because of Christ's life and death on their behalf, their lives would overflow with acts of service that were driven or motivated by the love of Christ.

In his book, *The Discipline of Grace*, Jerry Bridges discusses this idea that the gospel is the only proper motivation for godly living. In speaking of 2 Corinthians 5:14 ("For the love of Christ controls us..."), he says, "Notice...what compelled or motivated Paul in such a strong manner. It was not a continual challenge to be more disciplined, or more committed, or more holy. Rather it was his constant heartfelt awareness of Christ's love for him."[1] For so many years I read this verse essentially backwards. I understood it to mean that my love for Christ was what controlled or drove my behavior. What Paul is saying here in 2 Corinthians and what he is emphasizing to the Galatians in 5:6 is that it is Christ's love for us that drives and motivates us. Ignition of the only engine appropriately able to drive righteous living is not some form of internal *combustion*, rather it is an inner *comprehension* of the magnitude and permanence of Christ's love for those who are His own. Paul tells the believers at Galatia that neither law keeping (circumcision) nor law breaking (uncircumcision) is of any value. Rather, he says, it is faith that expresses itself through love.

Luke 18:9-14

And He also told this parable to certain ones who trusted in themselves that they were righteous, and viewed others with contempt: "Two men went up into the temple to pray, one a Pharisee, and the other a tax-gatherer. The Pharisee stood and was praying thus to himself, 'God, I thank Thee that I am not like other people: swindlers, unjust, adulterers, or even like this tax-gatherer. I fast twice a week; I pay tithes of all that I get.' But the tax-gatherer, standing some distance away, was even unwilling to lift up his eyes to heaven, but was beating his breast, saying, 'God, be merciful to me, the sinner.' I tell you, this man went down to his house justified rather than the other; for everyone who exalts himself shall be humbled, but he who humbles himself shall be exalted."

In this gospel account, Luke records the story of the Pharisee and the tax collector for us. In this passage Jesus is addressing "certain ones who trusted in themselves that they were righteous and viewed others with contempt" (v.9). From this reference we recognize that Jesus is speaking to those who are either positionally or functionally living on the upper left side of the Fork Illustration. He tells the parable of two men who go into the temple in Jerusalem to pray. One of them is a religious leader, a Pharisee, and the other is a tax gatherer. Tax collectors were despised by the Jews of the day for three reasons. First of all, they worked for Rome, the oppressive political power that had subjected the Jewish nation. Their job entailed collecting duties that were used to further advance the Roman Empire and strengthen the very government that held the Jews under its dominion. Secondly, most tax collectors would exact a greater amount from the public than dictated by Rome and retain the excess for personal profit. An additional reason the Jews had for disdaining tax collectors had to do with Jewish law. For Roman tax collectors to exact money from the people, they needed an accurate roll of all individuals living in their regions. To obtain such a roll, a census needed to be taken. Jewish law (1 Chronicles 21:1-8) forbade the Jews to take a census apart from the command of God.[2] With these factors as evidence, tax-gatherers were judged by the Jews to be incredibly licentious. We can view the lifestyles of these two individuals on the Fork as follows:

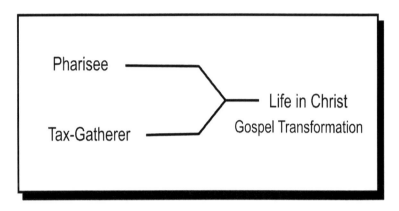

Pharisee

Tax-Gatherer

Life in Christ
Gospel Transformation

Along with the Jews, we infer that the tax collector lived what we would call a licentious life. He, in essence, stole from citizens through the use of his appointed office. On the other hand, the Pharisee was a man who is described by Jesus as going into the temple to pray "to himself." His unconscious desire was to be his own Savior. His lifestyle is contrasted with the tax collector. The Pharisee probably did give a tenth of his income to the temple and fast twice a week. He probably was very righteous in his external behavior. But he believed that he had a righteousness to recommend Him to God. He had obtained this righteousness by not disregarding the law like other people (v.11), who were "swindlers, unjust, adulterers, or even like this tax gatherer," but by fulfilling the law (v.12), by fasting twice a week and by tithing all that he got.

Jesus concludes the parable in verse 14 by saying, "I tell you, this man (tax gatherer) went down to his house justified rather than the other (Pharisee); for everyone who exalts himself shall be humbled, but he who humbles himself shall be exalted."

In this account we have the prayer of the tax gatherer. It deserves comment because it is such a perfect picture for us of what movement on the Fork looks like. The tax gatherer's attitude demonstrates movement from the left side of the Fork to the right. This movement is repentance and faith. We will look at this movement in more detail in Chapter 4, but for now, let's explore how repentance and faith are seen in the words of the tax collector.

We have to begin by getting into the world of the tax collector. Remember that this man was a Jew. We know this because the text tells us that he was in the temple praying along side of the Pharisee. As it is highly unlikely that this Pharisee would have stopped to pray in the Court of the Gentiles, the area of the temple designated for worship by those who were not of the nation of Israel, we can be fairly certain of the assumption that the tax collector was a Jew. As such, this man would have known the Old Testament writings of the law and prophets. He would have understood that there was a system of blood sacrifices necessary to approach a holy God. He would have been well versed in the ceremonial rituals concerning the tabernacle and the Holy of holies, that sacred place where only the High Priest of Israel was allowed to enter once a year to offer a sacrifice of atonement for the sins of the nation of Israel. He also would have known that the Ark of the Covenant was to be in the Holy of holies.

Now the ark was a wooden box that God had commanded Moses to construct. It was covered with gold and had a cover on top. This lid or cover was called "the Mercy Seat." On the Mercy Seat were two cherubim (angels) that were facing each other with their wings outstretched (Exodus 25:10-22). This was to be the place of God's presence with Israel (verse 22). In addition, the tax collector would have known what was *in* the ark, the second set of stone tablets that Moses had received from God on Mount Sinai (Deuteronomy 10:3-5).

When commenting about the ark and the Mercy Seat, James Montgomery Boice says, "...the ark is a picture of terrible judgment...for what does God see as He looks down upon earth from between the outstretched wings of the cherubim? Clearly, He sees the law of Moses, which each of us has broken."[3]

For God's righteous anger over Israel's rebellion against His law to be assuaged, on the Day of Atonement, an animal was killed and the blood brought into the Holy of holies and sprinkled onto the Mercy Seat by the High Priest. Boice goes on to say, "Now, as God looks down from between the outstretched wings of the cherubim, He does not see the law of Moses that has been broken, but instead He sees the blood of the innocent victim."[4] Punishment had been exacted and God's wrath was turned away.

Now, how is this all related to the tax collector's prayer, and what does it teach us about movement from the left to the right side of the Fork Illustration? Most of our modern translations render the prayer of the tax gatherer, "God be merciful to me, the sinner." In fact, the word translated here from the original language as "merciful" is the Greek word *hilaskomai*. There is some debate over this word's translation. While some feel that it should be rendered "expiate," most feel the better translations is "propitious," which means "to make propitiation." Propitiation is a word unfamiliar to most moderns, which is probably why most of our translations chose to use "merciful." Propitiation means "to turn away wrath." It assumes that there is an injured party who has the right to be angry. When taken as "propitious," the word is rich with temple sacrificial system imagery. The word *hilaskomai* can be understood to mean "to be Mercy Seated." So in essence what the tax collector says is, "God, be Mercy Seated toward me, the sinner." The text tells us that he stood at a distance, away from God in humility and repentance. What he did was amazing. This tax collector, understanding the pictures of the temple sacrificial system, pled the blood of an innocent sacrifice on his behalf. He believed himself to be guilty before God whose wrath was justified and in need of an atoning sacrifice. At the same time, he acknowledged by faith that such a sacrifice would be provided for him. He believed that with the blood of the lamb shed on his behalf and poured out for him, God could look down on him and no longer see a lawbreaker who was unable to keep what was written on those stone tablets. God's anger could be turned away on the basis of that sacrifice and he could have peace with God. This tax collector was pleading for God to "treat him on the basis of the blood sprinkled on the mercy seat" and he moved from the domain of darkness to the Kingdom of Light.

So while it may appear, by a literal reading of this parable in English, that the tax collector is merely asking for mercy, we see that he is actually not only repentant and indeed asking for forgiveness, but there is also the element of faith in his request that God be Mercy Seated toward Him.

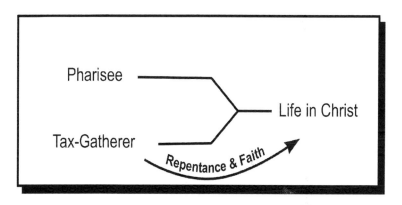

This is why Jesus holds him up as an example of one who "went down to his house justified." To use the language of the Fork, he "went over to the right justified." He renounced his flesh, despairing of any ability to save or wisely rule himself. He was transformed by the knowledge that he was completely sinful yet fully loved by God.

As believers we live positionally on the right side of the Fork. But because we spend so much of our lives functionally living on the left, we will later look at how movement from the left side of the Fork to the right similarly occurs in the life of a believer.

Luke 7:36-50

Now one of the Pharisees was requesting Him to dine with him. And He entered the Pharisee's house, and reclined at the table. And behold, there was a woman in the city who was a sinner; and when she learned that He was reclining at the table in the Pharisee's house, she brought an alabaster vial of perfume, and standing behind Him at His feet, weeping, she began to wet His feet with her tears and kept wiping them with the hair of her head, and kissing His feet, and anointing them with perfume. Now when the Pharisee who had invited Him saw this, he said to himself, "If this man were a prophet He would know who and what sort of person this woman is who is touching Him, that she is a sinner." And Jesus answered and said to him, "Simon, I have something to say to you." And he replied, "Say it, Teacher." "A certain moneylender had two debtors; one owed five hundred denarii, and the other fifty. When they were unable to repay, he graciously forgave them both. Which of them therefore will love him more?" Simon answered and said, "I suppose the one whom he forgave more." And He said to him, "You have judged correctly." And turning to the woman, He said to Simon, "Do you see this woman? I entered your house; you gave Me no water for My feet, but she has wet My feet with her tears, and wiped them with her hair. You gave Me no kiss, but she, since the time I came in, has not ceased to kiss My feet. You did not anoint My head with oil, but she anointed My feet with perfume. For this reason I say to you, her sins, which are many, have been forgiven, for she loved much; but he who is forgiven little, loves little." And He said to her, "Your sins have been forgiven." And those who were reclining at the table with Him began to say to themselves, "Who is this man who even forgives sins?" And He said to the woman, "Your faith has saved you; go in peace."

Here we have the account of a certain Pharisee named Simon who invited Jesus to have dinner with him. He enters Simon's house and reclines at the table. A woman of the city, a prostitute, comes into Simon's house, most assuredly uninvited, and brings a vial of perfume. She weeps at His feet, wetting them with the oil and her tears and then dries His feet with her hair. We are told in the text that the Pharisee observed this and thought to himself, "If this man were a prophet He would know who and what sort of person this woman is who is touching Him, that she is a sinner." Then Jesus proceeds to tell Simon a parable. The parable is about a moneylender to whom two individuals owed money. One debtor owed him 50 denarii and the other 500. Neither could pay, so the moneylender graciously forgives them both the entire debt. Then Jesus questions Simon, "Which of them therefore will love him more?" Simon properly replies that the one who had the larger debt would be more grateful, and Jesus tells him that he has answered correctly. Then Jesus goes on to point out that the parable is a picture of Simon himself and the prostitute. He gently rebukes Simon for not extending to Him even the most basic common courtesies of the time. He concludes by telling Simon that her sins, though many, have been forgiven, for she loved much, but that he who has been forgiven little, loves little.

I cannot do a better job of explaining this passage to you in light of the two faces of the flesh illustrated on the left side of the Fork than Josiah Bancroft does in the World Harvest Mission's Sonship course. He says,

> ...I want to contrast these two folks in their response to Christ.... Which one of these two people had faith expressing itself in love (Galatians 5:6)? Well it wasn't Simon, was it? It was the woman. Both of them sinners. Both of them illustrating these two faces of the flesh. The one, the sensualist. The other, the self-righteous. The one who is caught in all sorts of license. The other who is caught up in a legal spirit. They both illustrate these two faces of the flesh. One of the advantages that the woman had, though, was that hers was recognized. She saw hers for what it was, didn't she? And she came for forgiveness to Christ and receiving that forgiveness, knowing by faith that she would receive, as she comes to Him, what is the outpouring of her heart? She loves Him, doesn't she? She loves Him with all of her heart. Now let me ask you, where in the Old Testament or where anywhere in the law does it say to weep at the feet of Jesus? Where does it say to do the exact things that she did? There's no rule book, is there? This passion in her heart, fed by the Holy Spirit, leads her creatively to acts of love that are appropriate. And, by the way, are bold. She wasn't wanted in that Pharisee's house. She wasn't on the guest list, I promise. The Pharisees would have crossed the road to keep the hem of their garments from touching the dust that her feet touched because they believed it would pollute them. And here comes this walking pollution factory into Simon's house; everything

that she touches has got to be ceremonially cleaned. So when she goes around and touches Jesus, what does Simon think? "Golly. If he were a man of God, he'd at least have a clue." But you know, Jesus knows something that Simon doesn't. And that is the forgiveness in that woman's heart had changed her. And what was the expression of that faith? Loved poured from her life to Christ. Forgiven much, love much. Love poured from her life. Which of them would love Him more? The one who had the bigger debt canceled. "Therefore, I tell you her many sins have been forgiven for she loved much, but he who has been forgiven little loves little."[5]

In Chapter One we looked at Galatians 5:6, where Paul says that the only thing that matters is faith expressing itself through love. The woman in the parable is a perfect depiction of this concept. Her behavior is a free and creative expression of the love within her heart for the One who has pardoned her. Her behavior is not dictated by rules nor limited to common courtesies of the day, but rather she is set free to go beyond traditional practices of hospitality to demonstrate the depth of her gratitude, love and devotion. The characters of the passage can be visually represented as follows:

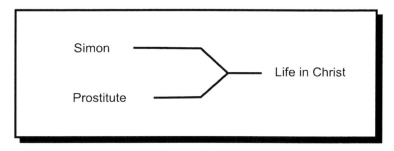

You see, there were at least two sinners in Simon's house that day. Both Simon and the woman were living in the flesh, on the left side of the Fork. But the amazing thing is that only the woman could see her need. This is a recurring pattern of which we should take note. It is easier for those who live licentiously to see their need of the grace of God than it is for those who live a life of legalism.

The licentious have the advantage of being able to recognize their sin and of seeing it for what it is. Yet the legalist seems to have his head buried in the sand and is oblivious to his real condition. Why is this true? Because the legalist who says, "I want to be my own Savior," is consumed with earning or maintaining a righteousness of his own. In pursuit of this righteousness, his focus is solely on those aspects of the law which he believes that he fulfills. He cannot allow himself to look at the demands of the law in areas where he knows he will not successfully uphold its standard of perfection.

Jonathan Edwards, a brilliant thinker and preacher of the 18th century, preached on the cyclical nature of law and grace.[6] By this he meant that we cannot let ourselves look at our sin, that is, to own up to it, unless we understand that there is grace available to cover that sin. Nor can we truly appreciate grace unless we see the magnitude and depth of our own sin. These two concepts have a symbiotic relationship. The more I see how sinful I am, the greater my appreciation for His grace to me. The greater my awareness of His grace, the quicker I am to run to Him in repentance for sins committed.

The legalist cannot let himself acknowledge his sin because he is unaware that grace is available to those who will admit inadequacy. He cannot "own up" to his shortcomings, failures, deficiencies and sin because he has nowhere to go with those feelings of insufficiency. Were he to claim his sin it would be an acknowledgment unto death and ownership unto annihilation. It is only when one understands that there is grace for the humble, for those who are willing to admit they are in need, that one can own up to his own faulty record and receive grace. James 4:6 says, "...God is opposed to the proud, but gives grace to the humble."

So many of us tend to view life on the bottom left side of the Fork, the licentious life, as worse than a life of legalism. The truth of the matter is that both a life of licentiousness and legalism are *equally* corrupt because neither is of faith. Romans 14:23 says, "...and whatever is not of faith [right side living] is *sin.*"

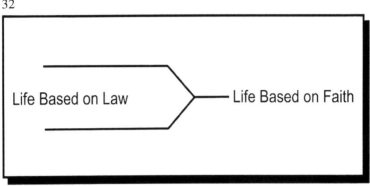

Life Based on Law ⟩——— Life Based on Faith

Yet why is it that there seems to be a greater tendency for repentance and faith from those who are on the bottom left side of the Fork rather than from those who are on the top left side? Think of the gospel message as a coin with two sides. One side is the part of the gospel message that is "bad news." This side tells us that we are totally sinful. The other side to the coin is the "good news." This side tells us that we are totally loved in Christ because He has atoned for our sin and imparts His perfect righteousness to us. Believers understand and accept both sides of this gospel coin. But now consider the licentious person. While this person may, because of his more obvious sin, readily see the "bad news" side of the coin, he rejects the "good news" side, that there is a Savior in whom is the perfect love and acceptance for which he yearns. Finally, consider the legalist. This person rejects both sides of the gospel coin. He rejects both the bad news of the gospel, assuming that he is not really all that sinful, and the good news of the gospel, because if he is not that sinful, he has no need of a Savior. So the reason the licentious person seems more likely to come into the Kingdom of God is because he has a vivid depiction of half of the gospel in his life. Now let me make sure that I stress this point. Both the legalist and the licentious person are equally lost because neither operates based on faith in the whole gospel message. Both are to some degree still trusting in "self." Unless both aspects of the gospel message are accepted by faith, an individual is still lost.

But even Jesus addresses this idea of the licentious being closer to the kingdom than the legalist when He spoke to the chief priests and elders of the Jewish nation in Matthew 21. In verses 31 and 32 He says to them, "Truly, truly I say to you that the tax-gatherers and harlots will get into the kingdom of God before you. For John came to you in the way of righteousness and you did not believe him; but the tax-gatherers and harlots did believe him; and you, seeing this, did not even feel remorse afterwards so as to believe him."

Now it is true that no one person is more lost than another. But it is interesting to note that some in Evangelical circles refer to the licentious as the "far lost" or those who are farthest from the Kingdom. This is a designation given, by some believers, to those who are non-churched. It is a classification for individuals who are prone to view all things spiritual or religious as irrelevant to life. Those who distribute this label believe that it is doubtful that the far lost would ever pass through the doors of any churches, Evangelical or otherwise. But if there were such a thing as "far" lost, the licentious would **not** be the ones who are the farthest away from the kingdom. The irony is that the actual "far lost" would be the legalists who see *neither* side of the gospel coin. This can be seen on the Fork as follows:

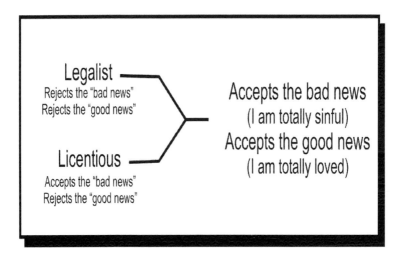

The licentious person has the advantage of having "obvious" sins of which he could more readily recognize and acknowledge and of which he can repent. The sin of the legalist is much harder to identify because outwardly he does all of the right things. The legalist is obedient, law abiding and does his duty. He works hard, and people respect and admire him. He is often religious and there is the possibility that he attends worship services, perhaps even regularly. Externally, his life may look faultless. From this position, it is more difficult for him or others to identify the sins and sin patterns in his life. He does not see the "bad news" and therefore, has no need for the "good news" either. It is his rejection of both aspects of the gospel that leads to the conclusion that if there were the possibility of a position further from the kingdom, it would be occupied by the legalist.

In this parable, the prostitute alone moves from the left side of the Fork to the right because she has acknowledged her sin, repented and believed in Christ as her Savior and Lord. Simon remains on the left, encased in his self-righteousness. He is either unaware of his sin, unable to own up to it due to an ignorance of the grace available to him, or unwilling to surrender his pride and ask for that grace. Because he was forgiven little, he loved little.

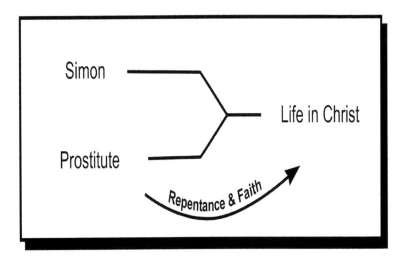

So often we are like Simon. According to Brennan Manning, "Many of us pretend to believe that we are sinners and consequently all we can do is pretend to believe that we're forgiven. As a result our whole spiritual life is pseudo-repentance and pseudo bliss."[7] On the other hand, this woman understood the reality of her sinful condition. As a result, she not only exhibited true repentance, but experienced the peace associated with knowing the forgiveness of the Lord.

Luke 15:11-32

And He said, "A certain man had two sons; and the younger of them said to his father, 'Father, give me the share of the estate that falls to me.' And he divided his wealth between them. And not many days later, the younger son gathered everything together and went on a journey into a distant country, and there he squandered his estate with loose living. Now when he had spent everything, a severe famine occurred in that country, and he began to be in need. And he went and attached himself to one of the citizens of that country, and he sent him into his fields to feed swine. And he was longing to fill his stomach with the pods that the swine were eating, and no one was giving anything to him. But when he came to his senses, he said, 'How many of my father's hired men have more than enough bread, but I am dying here with hunger? I will get up and go to my father, and will say to him, "Father, I have sinned against heaven, and in your sight; I am no longer worthy to be called your son; make me as one of your hired men." ' And he got up and came to his father. But while he was still a long way off, his father saw him, and felt compassion for him, and ran and embraced him, and kissed him. And the son said to him, 'Father, I have sinned against heaven and in your sight; I am no longer worthy to be called your son.' But the father said to his slaves, 'Quickly bring out the best robe and put it on him, and put a ring on his hand and sandals on his feet; and bring the fattened calf, kill it, and let us eat and be merry; for this son of mine was dead, and has come to life again; he was lost, and has been found.' And they began to be merry. Now his older son was in the field, and when he came and approached the house, he heard music and dancing. And he summoned one of the servants and began inquiring what these things might be. And he said to him, 'Your brother has come, and your father has killed the fattened calf, because he has received him back safe and sound.' But he became angry, and was not willing to go in; and his father came out and began entreating him. But he answered and said to his father, 'Look! For so many years I have been serving you, and I have never neglected a command of yours; and yet you have never given me a kid, that I might be merry with my friends; but when this son of yours came, who has devoured your wealth with harlots, you killed the fattened calf for him.' And he said to him, 'My child, you have always been with me, and all that is mine is yours. But we had to be merry and rejoice, for this brother of yours was dead and has begun to live, and was lost and has been found.' "

The text that is most easily understood on the Fork Illustration is the parable of the prodigal son. In it, the two faces of the flesh are clearly seen in the two sons. The younger son represents the licentious life. He goes to his father and requests his inheritance and then proceeds to squander all of it on "loose living." The older brother lives the life of the legalist. He remained at home and performed all that was expected of him.

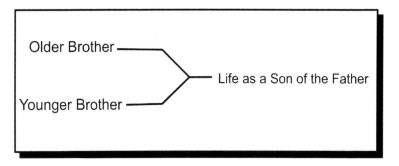

Older Brother — Life as a Son of the Father
Younger Brother —

Neither of these men was living as a "son" of the Father. One had openly rejected the father and his love. His request for his inheritance was the ultimate renunciation of their relationship. In *The Return of the Prodigal Son*, Henry Nouwen cites a work by Kenneth Bailey, which states that for the younger son to request his inheritance while the father was still alive, was equivalent to wishing for his father's death. Nouwen also says that the younger son's leaving was "...much more offensive than it seems at first reading. It is a heartless rejection of the home in which the son was born and nurtured and a break with the most precious tradition carefully upheld by the larger community of which he was a part."[8] In a sermon on The Prodigal Son, Dr. Timothy J. Keller explains that the younger son's request was selfish and brought injury to the entire family in numerous ways. The young man's request wounded the family *spiritually* due to the pain commonly associated with rebellious children. In addition, his petition damaged the family *economically*. In order to grant the request, the father would probably have had to liquidate many assets to give the son his inheritance in currency. The son's inconsiderate appeal also shamed the entire family *socially*. All business in that culture and period of time was conducted at the city gate. The father would have had to go to the gate and seek to sell possessions before the elders of the city. As the entire community discovered the reason for the sale, the family would have been humiliated. The family would also have been affected *physically* because there would now be fewer resources to provide for the basic needs of food, clothing, medicine, etc. for virtually the same number of people. Finally, Dr. Keller mentions that the father himself would have been *emotionally* wounded. The demand of the son for his inheritance would have been like a knife to the father's heart.[9] Whenever one lives in the "far country" there are consequences that affect not only the licentious person himself, but those around him as well.

The older brother was equally distanced from his father. Of the older brother, Henry Nouwen says, "Not only did the younger son, who left home to look for freedom and happiness in a distant country get lost, but the one who stayed home also became a lost man. Exteriorly he did all the things a good son is supposed to do, but interiorly, he wandered away from his father. He did his duty, worked hard everyday and fulfilled all his obligations but became increasingly unhappy and unfree."[10] Deluded in his belief that he is upholding the requirements of the law, the older brother is self-righteous and lives enslaved to bitterness, resentment and anger. He has no intimate relationship with his father. There is neither loving closeness nor trust in his familial bond.

In this section of Luke's gospel Jesus presents three stories: the Lost Coin, the Lost Sheep and the Prodigal Son. It is interesting to note the audience to whom Jesus is speaking this set of parables. Jesus is addressing a group consisting of (vv.1 and 2) "tax gatherers and sinners...and Pharisees and scribes." He is teaching those living on both prongs of the left side of the Fork. It can be represented as follows:

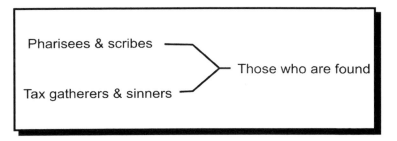

Because He is aware of His audience, He shows that both positions are wrong. One condition is not better than the other. Again, Henry Nouwen states it masterfully. He says, "This is not a story that separates the two brothers into the good one and the evil one. The father only is good. He loves both sons. He runs out to meet both. He wants both to sit at his table and participate in his joy."[11] Henry Nouwen makes the point that both sons were equally sinful in living autonomously from the father, yet the father faithfully pursues both with his love.

The point that is critical for us as believers to see here is that every time we search for unconditional love where it cannot be found, we have gone off to the far country. We, in essence, take our inheritance, who we are and all the riches that we have, and squander them. Although we have the status of sons who are positionally on the right side of the Fork, we become prodigals who have moved ourselves to the far country – life on the left. We are functionally living apart from our father and have forgotten our identity as his children. This movement comes so easily to us that it could almost be called our "default." We are so quick to forget who we are "in Christ" and where our true home is.

My mother is in the latter stages of Alzheimer's disease. When I recently spent time with her, she repeatedly asked to "go home." As we were in her home, the one in which she has lived for the last 41 years, I had to continually stimulate her memory with prompts of, "Mom, you *are* home," or "This *is* your home." She needs to be constantly reminded so that she can "come to her senses." I have come to the conclusion that we have spiritual Alzheimer's disease. Our hearts continually cry out, "I want to be loved. I want to be somebody." The Spirit of God bears witness to us, just as I did to Mom, that we *are* loved and that we are *so significant* that God was willing to sacrifice what He loved most, His Son, for us. But also just like my mother, we need unceasing reminders that He is our Father because we forget as soon as we've been told. This is the ministry of the Holy Spirit in the life of believers (Chapter 4). I think that the Apostle Peter knew about spiritual Alzheimer's long before Dr. Alois Alzheimer ever identified the neuritic plaque and neurofibrillary tangles in the brain that are factors of physical memory loss. In II Peter 1:10-15, he states that he wants the believers in Asia Minor to be certain of God's calling and choosing of them. Peter says,

> Therefore, brethren, be all the more diligent to make certain about His calling and choosing you; for as long as you practice these things you will never stumble; for in this way the entrance into the eternal kingdom of our Lord and Savior Jesus Christ will be abundantly supplied to you. Therefore, I shall always be ready to **remind** you of these things, even though you already know them, and have been established in the truth which is present with you. And I consider it right, as long as I am in this earthly dwelling, to stir you up by way of **reminder**, knowing that the laying aside of my earthly dwelling is imminent, as also our Lord Jesus Christ has made clear to me. And I will also be diligent that at any time after my departure you may be able to **call these things to mind.** (Italics mine)

Peter knew that no sooner are we reminded of God's calling and choice of us than those truths slip from our memory. He was not afraid to constantly remind the early church of the message of the gospel. When we are reminded of the truth and determine to return home, we are then faced with the decision of "how" we will return.

Once we "come to our senses" and realize that we are living in the far country, we have a tendency to do exactly what the younger son did. Rather than come back home and repent and believe that we have a father who is longing for our return, who loves us and wants only to receive us home as his sons, we often seek to take the wrong road home. We, like the prodigal, attempt to return home as "hired servants." A movement from the bottom of the left side of the Fork to the top left illustrates this.

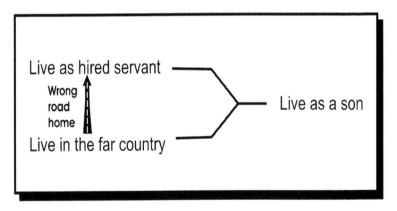

In Chapter 1 we called this a movement from "moral rebellion" to "moral reformation." What we need to remember is that the father did not allow the prodigal to travel this road home. In the passage, the younger son is said to "come to his senses." In his heart he decides that he will go back home to his father. He has planned out what he intends to say to him (verse 18), "Father, I have sinned against heaven and in your sight; I am no longer worthy to be called your son; make me as one of your hired men." He wanted to fix one aspect of his flesh by exercising the other. In Chapter One, we discussed the inability of the law to change us or solve our sin problem. We saw that law has no power to fix licentiousness because the law was not given nor designed to save, but only to point to our need of a Savior. So when we get to verse 21, we note that Jesus said the son's words were, "Father, I have sinned against heaven and in your sight; I am no longer worthy to be called your son." Before he can say anything further, the father is calling for the servants to bring the best robe, a ring and sandals, and to kill the fattened calf for a celebration. The son is not given the opportunity to add, "Make me as one of your hired men." The robe, ring and sandals were outward representations of this man's status as the father's son. The father's desire was not to punish, belittle, or demand penance from the son. It was solely to remind the young man of his sonship. He wanted the prodigal to realize who he was. His objective was to visually illustrate the prodigal's true identity with tangible reminders of his position and status as a son. When we live on the right side of the Fork we comprehend who we are and live out of our identity as children of God. The only road that truly leads home is this movement:

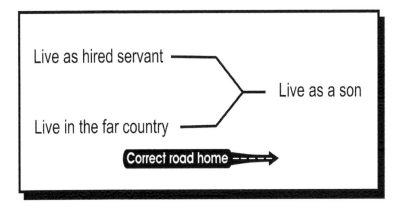

We earlier identified this movement as "gospel transformation." On this road we cover the territory of being reminded of our destitution but also that the Father is waiting at the path's end to race out and embrace us.

Colossians 2:16-23

The Apostle Paul clearly understood and explained to those in Colossae that moral reformation, attempting to fix licentiousness with legalism, as the prodigal was planning to do, would not work. Paul could have easily had the Fork Illustration in mind when he wrote the admonition in Colossians 2:16-23. To understand these verses, we need to look at what was going on in the church at Colossae and Paul's purpose in writing those believers. The church in that city was largely composed of converts from the Gentile world. Within this region was widespread paganism. The converts had come from worship of deities such as Demeter and Artemis or Helios and Selene.[12] Because of this background, there was danger of their returning to their former lives of pagan licentiousness. To combat this threat, false teachers in the church were encouraging these believers that they could have victory over their former lifestyle of "fleshly indulgence," yet they presented the wrong solution. Their message was that faith in Christ was fine, but not sufficient. The content of the epistle leads us to assume that they claimed that Christ was not a complete Savior, and that the Colossian believers needed to follow certain rules and regulations in order to have full knowledge, power to change, holiness and joy. These teachers promoted law keeping, along with believing, as the means to obtain a salvation that was full and complete. Their teachings "...attached special significance to the rite of physical circumcision, to food-regulations, and to the observance of such special days as pertained to the economy of the old dispensations."[13] They also included angel worship and Asceticism, an extremely harsh or severe treatment of the physical body. Webster's dictionary defines asceticism as the belief that one can reach a higher spiritual state by rigorous self-discipline and self-denial.[14]

With this in mind, we look at Colossian 2:16-23.

> Therefore let no one act as your judge in regard to food or drink or in respect to a festival or new moon or a Sabbath day--things which are a mere shadow of what is to come; but the substance belongs to Christ. Let no one

keep defrauding you of your prize by delighting in self-abasement and the worship of angels, taking his stand on visions he has seen, inflated without cause by his fleshly mind, and not holding fast to the head, from whom the entire body, being supplied and held together by the joints and ligaments, grows with a growth which is from God. If you have died with Christ to the elementary principles of the world, why, as if you were living in the world do you submit yourself to decrees such as, "Do not handle, do not taste, do not touch!" which all refer to things destined to perish with using-in accordance with the commandments and teachings of men? These are matters which have, to be sure, the appearance of wisdom in self-made religion and self-abasement and severe treatment of the body, *but are of no value against fleshly indulgence.* (emphasis mine)

Can you see what Paul is saying here? Let's put it on the Fork and then explain it.

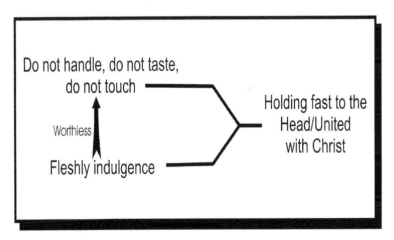

Do not handle, do not taste, do not touch

Worthless

Fleshly indulgence

Holding fast to the Head/United with Christ

Paul is reminding those who fall into indulgence of the flesh that moral reformation, attempting to use rule keeping to change or transform your character, is worthless. He rhetorically asks them why, if they are united to Christ through His death, would they want to submit themselves to laws such as, "Do not handle, do not taste or do not touch." He points out that while this may appear to be wise, this self-made religion and severe treatment of the body *is of no value against licentious living.* Paul is saying that you can't fix licentiousness with legalism. Legalism is of no value against license.

On March 20, 2003, the United States declared war on Iraq. Initial air strikes were made by the U.S. Air Force on Presidential Palace Complexes in Baghdad. These Presidential Palaces were known to contain underground bunkers capable of withstanding massive explosions. Specific munitions were needed to penetrate these subterranean facilities. Were the Air Force pilots to use bombs that detonate on impact in their assaults on these compounds, the bombs would most likely cause noticeable destruction at a surface level. The damage might even be assessed as remarkable. Yet the enemy within would remain unscathed. For the enemy to be destroyed the appropriate weapon must be utilized. Air Force personnel were directed to release "bunker buster" bombs that would infiltrate these buried fortresses and annihilate enemy strongholds. When we apply the law to our hearts in an attempt to remove legalistic behaviors, we are using the wrong weapon. While application of the law might produce noticeable or even remarkable surface change, our ultimate objective of enemy eradication remains unfulfilled. We need a bunker buster that will penetrate the stronghold and destroy the enemy within. God has placed such a weapon at our disposal. It is the gospel of grace. Only the gospel can penetrate our hard hearts. The gospel descends to a level that the law cannot and is the only effective means for eliminating licentious behaviors of our flesh.

In this passage, Paul is saying that you can't fix the left bottom tine of the Fork with the top left tine. He knew that the answer to licentious living was to hold fast to the Head, Christ. Being reminded of our union with Christ and resulting position as sons of the Father, just as the Prodigal Son was, is the only solution and the exclusive road that leads home. Self-reformation through law keeping is not the same thing as being transformed by the message of the gospel.

Am I saying that the law of God is useless or, even worse, evil? Of course not. In Romans 7 Paul says, "What shall we say then? Is the Law sin? May it never be! On the contrary, I would not have come to know sin except through the Law...." God gave us the law for specific purposes, one of which is to highlight for us our need for Christ. When we seek justification from law keeping, we misuse it. We circumvent the very function for which God designed it. When the law begins to convict us, everything within cries out for deliverance. Our problem is that one of the first places to which we look for rescue is the law itself. When we do this, we are looking to the law to be our Savior. Law was not given to be our Jesus, but rather to lead us to Him.

"The law was added so that transgression might increase" (Romans 5:20). The words "was added" actually mean "to enter along side of." The question that begs to be asked here is, "along side of what?" What did law come along side of? Law entered along side of sin that man already possesses in Adam. Law does not cause sin, but it does something to it. It exposes sin. And when sin is exposed, man is able to recognize the seriousness of his alienation from God. He can acknowledge that he not only needs help, but he desperately requires complete deliverance apart from anything he can manufacture on his own. So a function of law is to reveal sin and expose our need of a Savior.

When God initially gave the law to Moses, it included commands regarding the sacrificial system. Because God knew of our inability to fulfill the demands of the moral and civil law, He simultaneously gave ceremonial law that included visual representations of His redemptive solution for sinful man. Blood atonement was depicted in animal sacrifices and pointed forward to the sacrifice of the Spotless Lamb of God who was coming to take away the sin of the whole world. Hebrews 9:22 reminds us that "...without the shedding of blood there is no forgiveness." The Apostle Paul also emphasizes the fact that law was given to point us to Christ when he writes to the Galatians, "Therefore the Law has become our tutor to lead us to Christ, that we may be justified by faith." Law can point us to Christ, but our justification is by faith alone.

In addition, the law is an expression of the righteous character of God. If you ask your children, "Why is murder wrong?", they may respond by saying that it is wrong because the Bible says so. While this is true, it is not the ultimate reason for defining murder as wicked. The fundamental reason why murder is wrong is that it is contrary to the character of God, who is perfect in every way. The law of God is what reveals His flawless character to us.

The law of God is also the standard or blue print of our design. It is like an owner's manual, or set of instructions for how a person can function most effectively. For example, when my sons purchased a Play Station II, it came with an owner's manual. In it there were directions for operation and warnings to prevent break down. If my sons disregard the directions, the system will not perform the functions that is was designed to execute. In their excitement, should the boys bypass reading the directions and immediately attempt to play games on the system, they will flounder and operate under a trial and error method. They may or may not eventually figure out how things appropriately work. If the boys fail to heed the warnings, complete system failure can be expected. It was not the intention of those who designed the Play Station II that it be compatible with water. After brushing their teeth, were my sons to spit in the top of the system, in essence using it like a sink, the system would experience total collapse. The boys would have violated the design as outlined in the manual. In the same way, the law of God is like an owner's manual for life. To the degree that our actions coincide with the intentions of the Designer, following His directions and heeding His warnings, our lives function more effectively and system failure is avoided.

While seeing Scriptural passages on the Fork Illustration helps us to get a more comprehensive picture of the concepts represented, looking at real life examples allows us to personalize them and see how they apply to our daily lives. In the next chapter we will look at several practical examples on the Fork, examining how and where we live.

48

Chapter 3
Practical Examples on the Fork

Now that we have looked at concepts represented on the Fork Illustration and examined a few Scriptural passages through its grid, let's move on and look at some practical examples from daily life. I have mentioned that as believers we are positionally on the right side of the Fork. Our problem is that we don't "stay" there. We forget who we are and we either travel to the far country of licentiousness or stay at home, equally removed from the love of our Father as legalists. In the introduction to this book, I mentioned that my husband and I have three sons. The Lord has blessed us with a home that has a wonderful basement playroom. As our sons have entered the teen years, the Lord has brought us into a whole new realm of sanctification as parents!

VIDEO EXAMPLE
One afternoon I heard disturbing sounds drifting up from the basement. I quickly descended the steps to the playroom to find one of my sons punching his brother. I was confronted with "licentious" behavior.

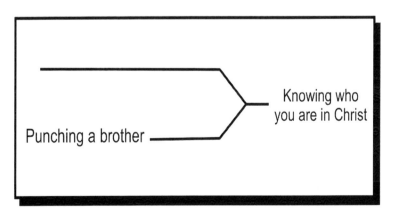

Now, why was one son, David, hitting Jeffrey, his brother? Jeffrey had deleted David's video game file, just when David had gotten to the point where he was about to beat the final "boss" or bad guy. What was motivating David's licentious behavior? In Chapter One, I mentioned that all behavior on the left side of the Fork is motivated or driven by fear, pride and belief in lies promoted by the world and the devil. The punching was motivated in part by fear. In his heart, David was telling himself, "I was about to beat the big boss. If I had beaten the big boss, then I would have something to recommend me to myself, others and God. Then I would be somebody. Now, since my file is gone, I'm nobody. I'll have to work harder to get back to the place where I was. I've lost valuable time in my journey to achieve video righteousness, and I must have that to make me acceptable." David's actions were driven by the fear that he would not earn or maintain significance. Since his brother had "stolen" that from him, he lashed out in anger. His behavior was also motivated by pride. His heart was boiling over with self-righteousness. "I can't believe that jerk deleted my file. *I* would never be that mean or inconsiderate to somebody else. I worked hard to get to that level in the game and I deserved to win. I deserved to keep *my* file." Finally, David is believing the lie that he must have a righteousness that comes from an ability to win at something. The world tells us that "winning" is where true significance comes from. The world whispers to us that if we want to be "somebody," we must be strong, wise, influential, powerful, rich – a winner. And David had listened to this voice.

So, what do most of us as parents do when confronted with a similar situation? Be honest! We enter into the conflict with a "Stop hitting your brother!" We come in and dump law onto our kids. Some of us are seemingly "holier" in our approach than other. Those who fall into that category come in and say, "Are you loving your brother? The Bible says, 'Little children, let us love one another.' Are you obeying the 'love one another' law? You should ask forgiveness and make up immediately!" While this might appear more "spiritual," it is still dispensing the law. This can be illustrated as follows:

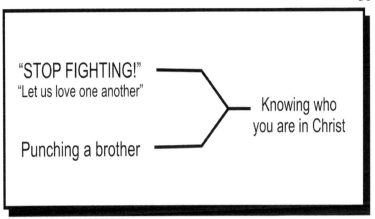

As a parent you have achieved a cease-fire, but at what cost? What is now motivating their behavior? Now they are "keeping the law." You have moved them from the bottom tine of license to the top tine of legalism, and we have already stated that this will not "fix" anything. The reason why this will not truly remedy the situation is because the motivation is still fear, pride and belief in lies of the world. Yes, you have altered their behavior in the short term, but fear and pride are motivating David's restraint of his anger. What is the new fear now driving his restraint? First of all, there is fear that if he does not cease and desist the physical violence, then Mom will deal with him. This could take the form of corporal punishment for smaller children or various forms of disciplinary intervention for older ones. Also, there can be fear that God will either be disappointed in him or actually punish him as well. So while the behavior has changed, the fear remains in the heart.

In addition to the fear, pride is also operating in the restraint of David's flesh. Perhaps as parents we have appealed to our children's pride by subtly instilling the idea that Christians are better than other people. Christians don't act that way. Christians are "above" that kind of behavior. C. S. Lewis explains this brilliantly in his book *Mere Christianity.* In the chapter entitled *The Great Sin,* he says this,

> Pride can often be used to beat down the simpler vices. Teachers, in fact, often appeal to a boy's pride, or, as they call it, his self-respect, to make him behave decently: many a man has overcome cowardice, or lust, or ill-temper by learning to think that they are beneath his dignity – that is, by pride.[2]

Or perhaps David recognizes that if he continues with the evidenced behavior and it becomes a pattern that he'll be labeled a "bully," and no one likes bullies. Bullies are almost as bad as those people who end up in jail; they're practically criminals! Bullies are shunned by "good" people. So again, while the behavior has been restrained, the pride in the heart remains. David remains on the left side of the Fork.

What can move him from the left side of the Fork to the right? The appropriate means of locomotion are the Spirit of God and the Word of God. The Spirit comes and through the use of the truth of the Word reminds us of our sonship. In this example, preaching 1 John 4:7 was described as using the law to drive my son deeper into the flesh. It just encouraged movement from license to legalism. I call this "driving them deeper into the flesh" because punching is an obvious sin that has a greater chance of being recognized and repented of than does self-righteousness or seeking significance apart from God. It is when we look at the rest of the passage that we see that verse 8 provides the proper and necessary motivation for movement to the right side of the Fork. 1 John 4:7-8 says, "Beloved, let us love one another, for love is from God; and everyone who loves is born of God and knows God. The one who does not love does not know God for God is love."

These verses tell us that love is from God. John reminds us that God loves us first. He initiates in our lives and we are completely loved by Him. How does this knowledge change our hearts and therefore our behavior?

There are two foundational truths of the gospel. One is that we are totally depraved. This is a fancy way of saying that I am sinful to the very depths of my being.

While it does not mean that I am as sinful as sinful can be, it does mean that my entire self is permeated with sin. Within my heart lies the ability to commit every sin. Even my best motives are tainted with self-interest. I am so sinful that God the Son had to come down to earth and die a criminal's death on a tree to pay the enormity of my debt. When I understand this, my heart is humbled. To admit to such deficiency and wickedness requires humility and brokenness. When I acknowledge the truth of this component of the gospel, my pride is broken. Pride in my life is not just rearranged or shuffled or manipulated. It is removed. Its stronghold is shattered. One manifestation of pride is not just substituted for another, as is the case when law alone is administered. David's pride manifested itself in self-righteous physical violence against his brother, but it also manifested itself in self-restraint in order to keep a holy reputation intact. The gospel is the only solution to his problem, because when he acknowledges the extent of his sinful condition, pride is broken. Pride is removed, not merely reconstructed or reorganized.

The second foundational truth of the gospel is that in Christ, we are deeply loved. When we are justified, we are united to Christ. Paul repeatedly speaks of our union with Christ in his epistles. He frequently uses the terms "in Him," "in Christ," "in the beloved," "with Him," and "united with Christ" to convey this idea to the believers of the early church. Because of our justification our sins have been forgiven and we have been clothed with Christ's innocence and righteousness. As such, when the Father looks at us, he sees Christ and, therefore, views us as "holy and blameless and beyond reproach" (Colossians 1:22).

My husband has a wonderful word picture of this that has helped many to understand the concept. I share it with you with his permission. Back in the 1960's, university fraternities practiced a ritual called "hazing." Hazing consisted of those who wished to join the fraternity undergoing various initiation rites. One of these was to require that a pledge swallow a live goldfish. If one were to look at the goldfish, all that could be seen would be the college freshman. My husband explains that we are like that goldfish. When we become Christians, Christ "swallows" us whole. Then when the Father looks at us, the fish within Christ's stomach, all He can see is Jesus. He sees Christ's perfectly lived life and He sees blood atonement for sin. All that is Christ is credited to us because we are "hidden in Him." Colossians 3:3 says, "For you have died and your life is hidden with Christ." Because of this the Father loves us just as He loves Jesus. Christ's sacrifice turned away the wrath of the Father. Therefore, having been justified by faith, we have peace with God (Romans 5:1). There is no condemnation for those who are in Christ (Romans 8:1). When I understand that the Father is not angry with me, that He always looks on me with love and favor just as if I were Jesus Himself, my fear is removed. I no longer have to fear punishment from God. I no longer have to fear His disapproval. Zephaniah 3:17 says that He rejoices over believers with shouts of joy. In Christ, the Father never looks at me with a frowning or angry countenance. There is always a look of delight and pleasure on His face, irrespective of my behavior, because He does not see me, He sees Jesus. He is never shaking His head nor "tsking" and clucking His tongue in disappointment. Isaiah 62:5 says that just as a bridegroom rejoices over the bride, so my God will rejoice over me. When these truths sink into my heart, all fear is removed. I realize that I am perfectly loved. The unconditional love that our hearts yearn for has been realized, and this is why the fear is removed. I John 4:18 says, "There is no fear in love; but perfect love casts out fear, because fear involves punishment, and the one who fears is not perfected in love." Only in recognizing the depth of the love of the Father for us can our fear be removed. One manifestation of fear is not merely substituted for another as in the example with my son. His fear manifested itself in lashing out against his brother and in harnessing his anger in outward law keeping. In both, the fear remained. It was just rearranged. Only at the Cross, only in remembering his identity in Christ can he remove the fear. In this example, as a parent I can come and enter into the conflict as an instrument of change in my son's life. I can point him to Christ and remind him of the gospel. Instead of merely administering law, I could say something like this, "David, because you are in Christ, God looks upon you with favor all of the time. He loves you perfectly and you do not need 'video righteousness.' You are 100% perfect in the eyes of the Father and there is nothing that you can do to add to 100%. And you are sinful. You have broken God's law in hitting your brother. You might think that you would never do what he has done to you, but you are also mean spirited and inconsiderate to others at times. You have 'deleted God's file.' You have broken His standards, yet instead of punching you, He punched Jesus on your behalf." Many times after such interactions I make this request of my sons, just to be sure they are "getting the message." "Show me the expression on God's face as He is looking at you right now." David understands what I am asking and always smiles. "Yes," I say, "God is indeed smiling. His face is radiant with delight as He is gazing at you, this and every minute, in Christ."

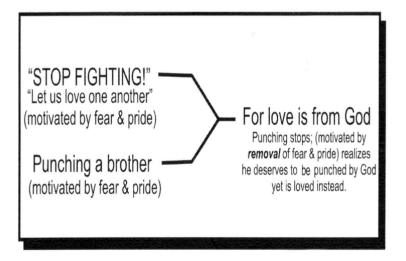

Without the gospel, we are simply trying to fix fear and pride with fear and pride. This results in a desperate existence that has deadly consequences. I came to understand these concepts from listening to the preaching of Dr. Timothy Keller, and it is directly from him that I borrow this terminology: "attempting to fix fear and pride, with fear and pride."[1] Let's look at another example that deals not with an external licentious behavior like punching, but an inner fleshly indulgence, like bitterness.

BITTERNESS EXAMPLE

Think of a time in your life when someone hurt you deeply through his or her lack of consideration, selfishness or anger. Perhaps someone has gossiped about you, and your reputation has been damaged. Perhaps they deceived or lied to you. Perhaps their actions hurt you financially. A lack of restoration in your relationship with that person has led you to harbor bitterness in your heart toward him. On the Fork, we can illustrate this as follows:

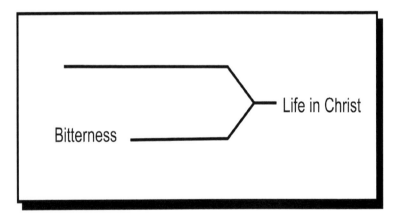

As a believer, the Holy Spirit is at work in you and convicts you, or brings to your attention the bitterness within. You think to yourself, "Yes, I am feeling bitter. I know that I shouldn't be bitter. Ephesians 4:31 says, 'Let all bitterness...be put away from you....'" So you remind yourself of the law and determine that you are no longer going to be bitter. "Christians are not bitter. Christians are loving people," you tell yourself. And you push the incident along with any thoughts of your brother into the back of your mind. You move on with the busyness of your life.

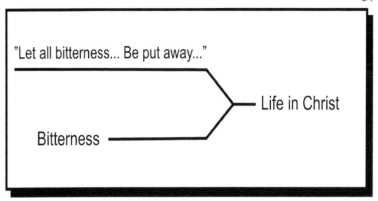

"Let all bitterness... Be put away..."

Bitterness ——————— Life in Christ

So now what happens? We mistakenly believe that real change has taken place in our lives. This fallacy is exposed when you next see or think of that brother. The memory of all that he has done to you and taken away from you returns and the bitter feelings resurface. You are still bitter. The reason for your continued bitterness is that you have not dealt with the fear and pride that is driving the bitterness. By reminding yourself of the law you are attempting to use a passing solution to fix a permanent problem. At one point or another in our lives, we have all experienced Post Nasal Drip caused by drainage dripping down the back of our throats. Suppose that you are in an important meeting and feel the drainage tickling your throat. You begin to cough to the degree that you are a spectacle. You tell yourself, "I will stop coughing! I will NOT cough," and then coughs seem to explode from your body with even greater force than before. You were trying to externally control or change something that had an internal cause. To control the coughing, the internal dripping must be dealt with. The same is true of us spiritually when we attempt to change a behavior with legalism or moral reformation. The inner problem, the *over* desires of our hearts that drive the "coughing," is still "dripping." When we try to stem the tide externally, often there is an even more extreme manifestation of the behavior than before the restraint. To control the "cough," an outside agent is needed who can deal with the root problem. We can go to the doctor or utilize cough drops or decongestants. In a like manner, to get rid of licentiousness, an outside agent, the Holy Spirit, is needed so that the root problem of idolatry can be healed.

Pride is the root or internal problem that has been driving your bitterness. *You* are wounded that someone has hurt *you*. They did not consider *you* and *your* feelings. They damaged *your* reputation. *You* feel that *you* deserve better treatment than this person has meted out to *you*. *You* could be ruined financially. Did you notice the number of times the pronoun "you" was used above. Many of us think that pride is an overly high opinion of ourselves. But pride can better be defined as an inordinate emphasis on self. This emphasis can take the form of either thinking we are "something" or of thinking we are "nothing." The point is that self is the focus of the thinking. Someone has wisely said that pr"I"de has an "I" in the middle of it.

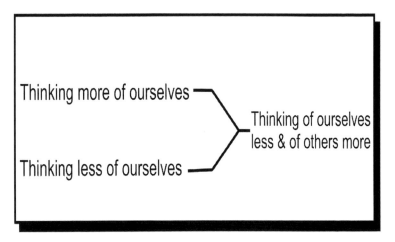

Thinking more of ourselves

Thinking of ourselves less & of others more

Thinking less of ourselves

The gospel is the permanent solution. Recognition of the depth of our own sin and the forgiveness that is ours in Christ coupled with the knowledge that we are completely accepted and provided for by the Father is the only solution for pride. When our pride is removed and fear is gone, we are finally free to think of ourselves less and others more.

Perhaps someone has lied to you. They have intentionally deceived you, exaggerated the truth, or not told you the whole truth concerning a person or event. When you discover the falsehood, you tell yourself, "I can't believe that someone could be so dishonest. I have been honest with him. I have treated him with respect." You tell yourself that you are so thankful that you do not treat others as he has treated you. "I could never be so despicable or lack integrity in that way!" Self-righteousness comes to us so easily and quickly. Just like a default on a computer, we seem programmed to compare ourselves with others in the areas where we delusionally think we perfectly fulfill the law ourselves. We view ourselves as "better," and pride is at the root of sustained bitterness.

Fear is also a root cause of ongoing bitterness. Licentiousness and legalism are always driven either by a heart that is consumed with self, or *afraid* it is insignificant. If this person's actions have diminished our reputation in some way, then we no longer have anything to recommend us; we have been devalued.

Deep within each human heart is the desire to "matter" to someone. We long to be seen as valuable and be loved by others. This is a God-given desire. He created us to be loved by Him, to matter to Him. If we do not know that we have the complete and irrevocable love of God, then we search endlessly for that love from others. In order to find that love, we must have an untarnished reputation, a basis upon which others may value us. To the same degree that our reputation is diminished, we lose self-worth and fear escalates.

Perhaps fear is driving the bitterness because your personal finances have been affected. You are experiencing anxiety over material resources. Each time you consider your financial position, you are confronted with tangible consequences of this person's actions. You fear that there will not be "enough" for you and your family. You are reminded that there will surely not be the "surplus" that you would have had apart from his sin, and bitterness results. You know that God calls you to release bitterness, but you just can't seem to make yourself change.

So we moved from the licentiousness of bitterness to the legalism of "Let all bitterness...be put away." Now we have fallen back into the licentiousness of bitterness again. Again, we recommit to the extermination of bitterness!

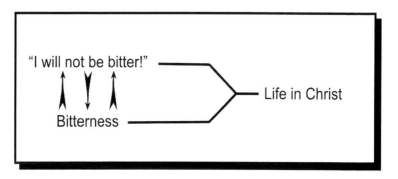

We attempt to use pride to motivate change by telling ourselves that we won't be bitter. We endlessly vacillate between the two faces of the flesh. We run back to legalism by telling ourselves, "I'm above bitterness, I'm a Christian. I refuse to be bitter and end up like those people who spend a fortune on psychiatrists and take anti-depressants or drink to oblivion. I'm a big enough person to just put it all behind me." We think of the Bible and remember Hebrews 12:15, "See to it that...no root of bitterness springing up causes trouble and by it many be defiled," and reason, "I'm more enlightened than those NT saints in the book of Hebrews. I have the whole counsel of God and I know better." We mistakenly assume that knowledge of the law is equated with understanding the truth of the gospel message and its application to the heart.

We are still living according to the flesh and our behavior is still being driven by pride. Our focus has become "lack of bitterness." This becomes our obsession. We are preoccupied and consumed with avoiding bitterness. Webster's dictionary states that to be consumed with something means to be "absorbed completely" by it.[2] Since we cannot be consumed with more than one thing, when avoiding bitterness is our obsession, Christ is not.

In addition, we allow fear to motivate our legalism along with this pride. We tell ourselves that God sets His face against those who won't forgive. We believe that God will punish us for a lack of forgiveness, so we tell ourselves that we must forgive. The medical profession tells us that bitterness can emotionally affect us to the point of harmful physical manifestations, so we determine to get the upper hand and master it. Fear is motivating a temporary change in outward behavior.

What is the solution? What has the power to break this vicious cycle of vacillation between the two faces of the flesh? As we saw in our previous "video" example, only the gospel of grace can set us free. The gospel deals with the fear and pride that motivates or drives all behavior under law.

In this example we looked at Ephesians 4:31, "Let all bitterness...be put away from you...." It is interesting to note that in the writings of the Apostle Paul, so often we find that when he reminds us of the law, he also reminds us of the gospel message of grace at the same time. Sometimes he tells us who we are in Christ, and then he says, "therefore," and reminds us of the holy character of God, which we are called to emulate. Other times, he directs our attention to our calling as saints and then reminds us of the engine that drives such behavior, the gospel of grace. Ephesians 4:31 & 32 are a perfect example of this second contingency. If, when we find ourselves struggling against bitterness and a lack of forgiveness, we simply remind ourselves of the law in verse 31, we will remain trapped in the cycle of vacillation between licentiousness and legalism. But if, when we are convicted of our bitterness, we hear Paul remind us of the gospel in verse 32 as well, we will be set free from the destructive pattern. Ephesians 4:32 says, "And be kind to one another, tender-hearted, forgiving each other, *just as God in Christ also has forgiven you.*" When we can "hear" the message that we have committed incalculable offenses against a holy God, but have been forgiven in Christ, only then are we able to let go of the bitterness and forgive a brother who has wounded us. We deserve God's "bitterness" toward us, but in Christ we only receive His favor and delight. On the Cross, Christ faced all of the bitterness of God on our behalf so that the Father need never harbor a grudge against us, ever. He never holds us at arm's length or requires "payback" from us as His offenders.

When we can wrap our minds and hearts around these truths, then we can repent of our bitterness and forgive completely. Does this mean that we'll never remember the offense of our brother again? Does it mean that the next time we look into our checkbook and see the obvious effects of his sin on the life of our family that we just pretend it never happened? No, what it does mean is that each time we are confronted with a reminder of that sin, we remind ourselves that we were willing to absorb the cost of that debt ourselves. We forgive as our Father has forgiven us. While Christ has paid our debt before the Father, who in our example has paid? If you have chosen to forgive, *you* have paid. You have decided to absorb the cost of a hurt that was minimal compared to the grief your sin affords the Father. Every time He gazes into His heavenly "checkbook" and is reminded of the consequences of our sin, the death of His Son, He could turn a bitter face toward us. Yet His facial expression is always one of love and delight when His eyes are trained on us. This is what the gospel message is all about. This is how we are enabled to move from the left side of the Fork to the right. This is what it means, in part, to live out of who we are in Christ. This is what it means to "live out of the gospel." And it is what it means to be transformed by grace.

Every indulgence of the flesh can be put on the Fork. Law can ineffectively address each of these licentious deeds. And each wicked act has a corresponding solution in the Cross of Christ. You could place "gossip" on the licentious tong and the reminder from Ephesians 4:29 that we are to "let no unwholesome word proceed out of our mouths..." on the legalistic tong. Then we can hear the good news of the gospel that because of Christ, while we deserve for God to shout out a listing of our sins to the universe, He only speaks well of us in Christ, always.

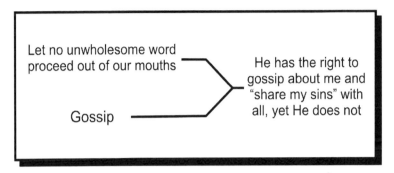

You could place "lust" on the licentious tong of the Fork and the words of law from 1 Corinthians 6:18 that we are to "flee immorality" on the legalistic tong. Then we can hear the words of Paul in 1 Corinthians 6:20 where he tells us, "For you have been bought with a price: therefore glorify God in your body." He reminds us that Christ loved us so much that He paid for us with His *life*. He willingly laid down His life when He did not have to. Are we really so foolish to believe that the person we are lusting after could or would love us like that?

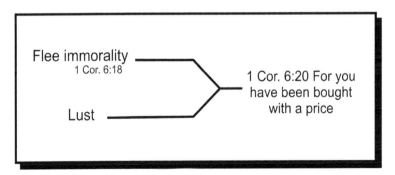

The point is that this gives you a model from which you can evaluate how you are seeking change in your life. Are you trying to externally reform your life through rigorous adherence to law, or are you allowing the gospel of grace to penetrate your heart and remake you from the inside out?

Let's move on and look at God's provision for enabling real and lasting heart change in our lives. How do we move from the left side of the Fork to the right? While it is true that this movement occurs initially, when we first place our trust in Christ, it also must occur daily as we move from living out of our flesh to living out of our identity as children of the King. Chapter 4 examines more specifically how the change takes place.

Chapter 4
The Holy Spirit on the Fork

What exactly is the ministry of the Holy Spirit? He is at work in the lives of both believers and non-believers. He has numerous responsibilities as the presence of God in the world today.

In evaluating modern Christians, J.I. Packer says this of their view of the Holy Spirit:

> Christian people are not in doubt as to the work of Christ. They know He redeemed men by His atoning death, even if they differ among themselves as to what exactly is involved. But the average Christian is in a complete fog as to what work the Holy Spirit does. Some talk about the Spirit of God in the same way one would talk about the spirit of Christmas. Some think of the Spirit as inspiring the moral convictions of unbelievers like Gandhi. But most, perhaps, do not think of the Holy Spirit at all and have no positive ideas of any sort about what He does. They are, for all practical purposes in the same position as the disciples who Paul met at Ephesus in Acts 19:2. (Acts 19:2 "...and Paul said to them, 'Did you receive the Holy Spirit when you believed?' And they said to him, 'No, we have not even heard whether there is a Holy Spirit.' ")[1]

What is the ministry of the Holy Spirit in the life of a believer? The Holy Spirit is, in part, our weapon of defense. He is like a rifle that we keep in our home to protect us against thieves who attempt to break in or against those who would seek to harm us. The problem with most Christians is that we don't know how to use our rifle. We can own a rifle, but if we don't know how it works, it is of little value to us when we are in eminent danger.

While we long to see change in our character and to be more conformed to the image of our Savior, we often live defeated lives. We believe the lie that Satan whispers to us that we'll never change. We live oblivious to the fact that our Father has given us the necessary Resource to change. We are so desperate in our need of that Resource that He had to place it inside of us so we could not remove ourselves from Him and His influence. We have an asset within that is of incalculable value, and we are ignorant of its worth.

In J.R.R. Tolkien's *Lord of the Rings* trilogy, Bilbo Baggins, a hobbit, gives his nephew Frodo a suit of armor prior to Frodo's leaving on a journey of destiny. Frodo puts this suit of armor on and then puts his old clothes over it. Frodo and his companions set out on their quest. At one point in the story they are walking along and his companions begin to talk about Bilbo and his adventures that brought him fame and riches. The company is traveling through the mines of Moria, the former home of the Dwarves. When asked why the Dwarves would want to return to mines that have been stripped of all gold and jewels, Gandalf, the leader of the troop replies,

> "For mithril... The wealth of Moria was not in gold and jewels, the toys of the Dwarves; nor in iron, their servant. Such things they found here, it is true, especially the iron; but they did not need to delve for them; all things that they desired they could obtain in traffic. For here alone in the world was found Moria-silver, or true-silver as some have called it: mithril is the Elvish name. The Dwarves have a name which they do not tell. Its worth was ten times that of gold, and now it is beyond price; for little is left above ground...All folks desired it. It could be beaten like copper, and polished like glass; and the Dwarves could make of it a metal, light and yet harder than tempered steel. Its beauty was like to that of common silver, but the beauty of mithril did not tarnish or grow dim...Bilbo had a corslet of mithril-rings that Thorin gave him. I wonder what has become of it?"
>
> "What?" cried Gimli (the dwarf), startled out of his silence. "A corslet of Moria-silver? That was a kingly gift!"
>
> "Yes," said Gandalf. "I never told him, but its worth was greater than the value of the whole Shire and everything in it."
>
> Frodo said nothing, but he put his hand under his tunic and touched the rings of his mail-shirt. He felt staggered to think that he had been walking about with the price of the Shire under his jacket. Had Bilbo known? He felt no doubt that Bilbo knew quite well. It was indeed a kingly gift.[2]

Gandalf is telling the group that for all of Bilbo's wealth, he had one possession that was worth more than all of his other assets combined. In fact, this one possession was worth more than the value of all the land of the Shire, the country where his people lived, plus the value of everything that was in it. That one possession was a suit of armor made entirely of mithril. As we read, mithril was the most valuable substance in Middle Earth. Mined by Dwarves, it was lighter, stronger and more beautiful than gold or any other substance. As Gandalf reveals this information to the troop of companions, all of a sudden, Frodo stops. He puts a hand to his chest and we can imagine his eyes growing large and his breath growing short. In that moment, he realizes and is overwhelmed at the enormity of the gift that his uncle has given him. It was a gift fit for a king. It was a possession of royalty, and he staggers at the thought that he is walking around wearing something of incredible worth underneath his old clothes.

As Christians, God has given us the Holy Spirit as we journey through this life. Underneath our old flesh, we are walking around "wearing" something of incredible value and most of us don't even know it. At best, most of us are ignorant of the worth of the Holy Spirit. At worst, we are completely oblivious to His existence and presence in our lives. If we really knew what we had, we would be staggered. We should be overwhelmed by this knowledge. When we contemplate the indwelling presence of the Holy Spirit it should make our eyes grow large and our breath grow short. As princes and princesses of the kingdom of heaven, we have been granted a gift fit for royalty. And there is no doubt that our Father is well aware that the Spirit is indeed a kingly gift.

Why is our perception of the Holy Spirit so important? If we recognize that He is a *person* and not an "it" and that He is powerful, then we can rely on Him. Just like we recognize Christ is a divine *person* and we rely on His work on our behalf, so too it is only when we see the Spirit as a person that we can rely on His ministry to us. Without a proper understanding of who He is and what He can do, we partially forfeit benefits that can come from His work on our behalf.

So what specifically is the ministry of the Holy Spirit? John 16:13-14 says, "But when He, the Spirit of truth, comes, He will guide you into all truth. For He will not speak on His own initiative but whatever He hears He will speak and He will disclose to you what is to come. He shall glorify Me for He shall take of Mine and disclose it to you." This tells us that the primary ministry of the Holy Spirit is to glorify Christ.

In his book, *Keep In Step With the Spirit*, J.I. Packer gives this wonderful word picture describing the ministry of the Holy Spirit.

> I remember walking to a church one winter evening to preach on the words "he shall glorify me," seeing the building floodlit as I turned the corner, and realizing that this was exactly the illustration my message needed. When floodlighting is well done, the floodlights are so placed that you do not see them; you are not in fact supposed to see where the light is coming from; what you are meant to see is just the building on which the floodlights are trained. The intended effect is to make it visible when otherwise it would not be seen for the darkness, and to maximize its dignity by throwing all its details into relief so that you see it properly. This perfectly illustrates the Spirit's new covenant role. He is, so to speak, the hidden floodlight shining on the Savior.[3]

Packer provides us with a powerful word picture that reminds us how very strange it would be for us to gaze upon an illuminated architectural masterpiece and remark, "My, what incredible lights! I wonder what the wattage is! I wonder how much electricity or power is required to produce that amount of light. Those lights are positioned at the perfect angle to the best cast light and shadows on the building." No! The purpose of the lights is to focus the attention of the viewer on the *building* itself. To bring the lights and their power to illuminate to center stage is to miss the point. This is, of course, analogous of the Holy Spirit, who illuminates Christ, the building, for us, the spectators. From this illustration we learn that the Holy Spirit does not speak of nor draw attention to Himself. Any emphasis on the person and work of the Spirit Himself that detracts from the person and work of Christ is not the intent of the Holy Spirit. Important as He is in glorifying Christ or making Him more clearly visible, the Holy Spirit is not to pre-empt the place of Christ in our thinking. By the same token, whenever Jesus is lifted up, glorified or exalted in any way, we can be sure that it is the result of the Holy Spirit's activity. Any time our thoughts reflect on Christ or we are reminded of Him, any time Christ is illuminated, it is because the Spirit has prompted that work in our minds and hearts.

So where do we find the Holy Spirit on the Fork? Although believers live positionally on the right side of the Fork, we forget that we are His and so easily revert back to life in the flesh. The ministry of the Holy Spirit is to move us from the left side, where we are functionally living either out of licentiousness or legalism, to the right side, where we see Christ and live out of our identity in Him.

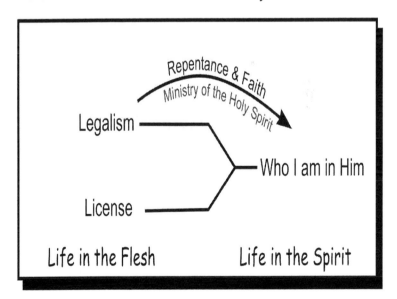

It is the Holy Spirit's ministry to enable us to repent and believe. He is the "warrior" Spirit who fights both against and for certain things in the hearts of believers. First of all, He fights against sin in us. He wages war against the flesh. Galatians 5:17 says, "For the flesh sets its desire against the Spirit and the Spirit against the flesh; for these are in *opposition* to one another so that you may not do the things that you please." If you are a Christian, the flesh and the Spirit are facing off on the battleground of your heart. They are in direct opposition to one another and there is no neutral ground. In every choice or decision we make, we either sow to the flesh or sow to the Spirit. We always choose sides, always.

It is important to note here that when this passage in Galatians mentions "flesh," it is not just talking about our skin or our physical selves. The Greek word that Paul uses here is *sarx.* In his book on the Apostle Paul, Herman Ridderbos describes Paul's use of the word flesh as follows:

> Flesh does not refer only to the physical, nor merely to the human as such, but to the human in its weakness, transitoriness, that which Paul elsewhere terms being "of the earth, earthly"...Flesh and spirit represent two modes of existence, on the one hand that of the old aeon which is characterized and determined by the flesh, on the other that of the new creation which is of the Spirit of God.[4]

Ridderbos is making the point that when the Apostle Paul uses the word "flesh," while it may refer to the physical nature of man, it encompasses much more. It refers to life apart from Christ as contrasted with a life abiding in Him. "Flesh" is that desire within man to be his own God and to live autonomously and independently from God. Here, it refers to both the desire within us to determine what we do, when we do it, how and with whom we do it and/or the drive within us to be self-sufficient, to never have to "need" anything from anyone, including God Himself.

And even though we have desires in our flesh that are driving and causing us to make wrong choices, decisions that dishonor the Lord, we also have the Spirit, who desires what is contrary to the flesh. Galatians 5:17 says that the flesh sets its desire against the Spirit and *the Spirit against the flesh.* What exactly does the Spirit of God desire in His antagonism against the flesh? He is jealous for the territory of your heart. James 4:5 in the New International Version says this: "Or do you think Scripture says without reason that the Spirit He caused to live in us envies intensely?" So the first battle of the Spirit is against sin.

But secondly, the Spirit battles *for* us. His goal is to glorify Christ (John 16:14). He continually seeks to remind us of who we are in Christ. We have been united to Christ as believers, yet we so quickly forget that truth. Colossians 1:23 says that we "move away from the hope of the gospel." A friend of mine loves to say that we have "Teflon-coated hearts." By this he means that the gospel message just slips right off the surface of our hearts. It just doesn't stick. We can be reminded of the message of grace and of our identity as children of the King and in the very next instant forget and need a fresh reminder. This is such a serious condition that God had to send His Holy Spirit to actually move in with us so that we could have constant reminders. He has to live inside of us, to dwell in our hearts.

My kids can remember this aspect of the ministry of the Holy Spirit when I call it His "Darth Vader" ministry. In the *Star Wars* movie series episode V, *The Empire Strikes Back,* there is a scene in which Darth Vader reveals his true identity as Luke Skywalker's father. In that wonderful voice of his, we can almost hear James Earl Jones enlighten Luke by saying, "I *am* your father!" So, too, the Holy Spirit lives within us and constantly says to us, "He *is* your Father." Scripture supports this in Galatians 4:4-6, where we read, "But when the fullness of time came, God sent forth His Son, born of a woman, born under the Law, in order that He might redeem those who were under the Law, that we might receive the adoption as sons. And because you are sons, God has sent forth the Spirit of His Son into our hearts, *crying, 'Abba! Father!'"* As the Spirit cries out, we are reminded that we are children of God. The Spirit reminds us that "He *is* your Father," and that as part of God's family He constantly delights in us. He brings to our remembrance the fact that we have the smiling countenance of a loving Father looking down on us continually. 1 Corinthians 2:12 reminds us, "Now we have received, not the spirit of the world, but the Spirit who is from God, *that we might know the things freely given to us by God"* (emphasis mine). This verse reminds us that the ministry of the Holy Spirit is to enable us to truly know the things freely given to us by God. We may know the truths of His choice and calling of us, our justification, our adoption and so on in our heads, but we need to know it more than just intellectually. We need to know it down in the depths our very being. We need to be reminded that while the things of God are freely given to us, they are extended at great cost to Him. We need to really know what we already know. Paul communicates this truth when he tells Timothy, "...*for I know whom I have believed* and I am convinced that He is able to guard what I have entrusted to Him until that day" (2 Timothy 1:12, emphasis mine). Paul says that he experientially *knows* what he believes.

How does the Holy Spirit do this? John 14:16-17 says that He guides us into all truth. The Spirit of God takes the word of God and brings to mind all of the things of Christ and the promises of the Father. We can think of all of the Scripture that we have "hidden away" (Psalm 119:11) in our hearts as a weapons arsenal of the Spirit of God. In his book *Grace Walk*, Steve McVey likens Scripture Memory to loading a gun. Taking the time to memorize and review the Word is our arming the Holy Spirit with ammunition. It is our chambering a bullet in a gun that He can use to defend us.[5] Most children raised in Evangelical churches are taught early on about the armor of God from the book of Ephesians. Ephesians 6:17 says, "...take the helmet of salvation and the sword of the Spirit which is the w*ord of God."* This verse likens the Word to a weapon. Time spent in the Word is analogous to our creating a munitions dump of sharp weapons for the Spirit to pull out when He needs some good hardware.

Let's catalog some of the possible firearms that we might have in our munitions dump.

- Romans 5:1 "Therefore, having been justified by faith, we have peace with God though our Lord Jesus Christ."
- Romans 8:1 "There is therefore now no condemnation for those who are in Christ Jesus."
- Romans 10:4 "For Christ is the end of the law for righteousness to everyone who believes."
- Romans 8:15 "For you have not received a spirit of slavery leading again to fear, but you have received a spirit of adoption as sons."
- Zephaniah 3:17 "The Lord your God is in your midst, a victorious warrior. He will exult over you with joy, He will be quiet in His love, He will rejoice over you with shouts of joy."
- II Corinthians 5:21 "He made Him who knew no sin to be sin on our behalf, that we might become the righteousness of God in Him."
- John 14:18 "I will not leave you as orphans, I will come to you."
- Ephesians 1:3,4 "Blessed be the God and Father of our Lord Jesus Christ, who has blessed us with every spiritual blessing in the heavenly places in Christ, just as He chose us in Him before the foundation of the world, that we should be holy and blameless before Him."
- Ephesians 1:7 "In Him we have redemption through His blood, the forgiveness of our trespasses, according to the riches of His grace."
- Galatians 5:1 "It was for freedom that Christ set us free...."

Obviously, I could go on and list verse after verse that reminds us of who we are in Christ and how we are viewed by the Father as a result of that union with Jesus. When these truths are hidden in our hearts, the Spirit ministers to us in times of temptation by "firing" these truths onto the front line of our minds. He makes them real to us and reminds us of what we already know. His desire is that we would experientially and applicationally know, in that moment, what we already intellectually know. We then can choose whether we will believe what God says is true or whether we will believe the lies of our enemies (Chapter 6).

The Holy Spirit seeks to keep before us, in graphic images, the person and work of Christ. He desires to keep Jesus center stage in the theater of our minds. The house lights of self must be extinguished and Christ must be the focus of all. Other voices that clamor for our attention must be unheeded or silenced. The Spirit must come and take the great truths of Scripture and make us intensely aware of them. He takes promises concerning God's calling and choice of us, promises explaining our justification, promises which remind us of our adoption into His family and passages detailing our union with Christ and our identity in Him and He causes them to become our reality.

As we intellectually process this, we acknowledge that this is indeed what we need. Yet how do we get more of the Holy Spirit's influence in our lives? Notice that the question is not , "How do I 'get more' of the Holy Spirit?" As mentioned at the start of this chapter, the Holy Spirit is a person, a whole person. And when we are justified, we get *all* of Him, forever. So how do we access or unleash His power within our lives?

Again, no one has given a more powerful illustration of this than Dr. Keller:

> I've had a number of Christians say to me, "I want the fullness of the Spirit, what do I do? It seems so mysterious. Do I have to open my hands...to get it? Do I have to sit and wait? Do I have to empty my mind? Do I have to submit? What do I have to do? Do I have to confess all known sin?" Now none of those things might be wrong, or even bad at all. But...listen, if you want to have a great evening with somebody, get him or her on a subject that he likes. If you want to have a great evening, find a subject that this person has a passion for and has expertise in and get on that subject, and you're off! And you're going to have a great evening. Do you want the fullness of the Spirit? I know His favorite subject, and so do you now. The thing, the topics, the truths that He is obsessed with...what He's passionate about....[6]

The Spirit is passionate about Jesus. His favorite topic is Jesus and what He has accomplished for us on the Cross. His obsession is telling of Jesus' amazing love and grace toward us. He is an expert on the life and ministry of Jesus. Dr. Keller goes on to say, "You read about those things. You meditate on those things. You talk to other friends about them...and you say, 'Spirit, make these things real. Show me these things...make them vivid realities.' That's how you seek the fullness of the Spirit. It is not an abstract thing."[7] Seeking the fullness of the Spirit is getting on our hearts what is on His heart, and that is the person and work of Christ. This is His passion. This is His obsession.

At the same time, we recognize that we can hinder or squash the influence of the Spirit within us. It makes sense logically that if His passion is Christ, then anything that is not of Christ or concerning Christ detracts from our being in step with the Spirit of God. If Christ is His favorite topic, when we focus our attention or direct our hearts' gaze on anything other than Jesus, we hinder the work of the Spirit. The Holy Spirit is grieved when we remove Jesus from center stage and head for the spotlight ourselves. The Spirit wants only Jesus to get all of the glory, ever. So whenever we boast, we direct the attention on us and we hinder the work of the Spirit.

So many of us think of boasting as speaking well of ourselves. This is a truncated and impoverished view of boasting. While boasting does include those times when we tell of our outstanding achievements and infamous accomplishments, it also includes any conversation that centers on "self." We do this so often and so easily with no conscious thought needed at all. For example, the new school year is starting and you are dropping your kids off at school that first morning. You see a friend with whom you've not had contact all summer. She comes over and you ask how her vacation was. She says, "Oh, we were able to take the kids down to Disney World and spend some time on the beach. It was wonderful." And then you say, "Really, we made it as far as Six Flags in Atlanta." While you have not sought to elevate yourself in terms of "outdoing" your friend in behavior or promote yourself as "better" in some way, you have turned the focus onto yourself, and this is boasting.

We so readily talk about ourselves. We are our favorite topic of conversation. Why are we so quickly bored when around people who constantly talk about themselves? Because the topic is not "us." This deep-seated obsession to be central is boasting.

In direct opposition to boasting is a broken and contrite heart. This is a heart that acknowledges that it can do nothing and bring nothing to God. It is a heart that is bankrupt of self and comes to God from a position of need. It is a humble heart whose focus is no longer self. And the only thing that is absolutely irresistible to the Spirit of God is a humble, broken and contrite heart. We are told in James 4:6 that "God is opposed to the proud, but gives grace to the humble." It is no coincidence that this verse follows the one mentioned above concerning the Spirit's jealously desiring the territory of our hearts.

Exactly how the Spirit works within to change us is found in 2 Corinthians 3:18. "But we all, with unveiled face beholding as in a mirror the glory of the Lord, are being transformed into the same image from glory to glory, just as from the Lord the Spirit." This verse tells us that we are changed in our character, by the Holy Spirit, through *beholding* or gazing. The more clearly we see Jesus, the more we will look like Him. The work of the Holy Spirit is to give us a clear representation of Christ.

1 John 3:1-2 says, "Beloved, now we are children of God and it has not appeared as yet what we shall be. We know that, when He appears we shall be like Him, because we shall see Him just as He is. And everyone who has this hope fixed on Him purifies himself, just as He is pure."

What is it about our arrival in heaven that will cause our flesh to finally and completely fall away? In our glorified state, we will no longer be able to sin. St. Augustine provided a clever way for us to remember man's relationship to sin in different conditions. He said that in the Garden of Eden, Adam and Eve were able not to sin. Fallen man is not able not to sin. Redeemed man is able to not sin. And glorified man is not able to sin. When we see God face to face, we will no longer be able to sin. Why is that? It is because our revelation of Him will be complete. We will behold Him as He really is, and when we do, it will thoroughly complete our transformation. The world tells us that we are changed by doing, by trying to change ourselves. The Word tells us that we are changed by beholding. The truths of the Bible are overwhelmingly radical and stand in direct opposition to the lies of the world.

Paige Benton, a popular speaker at women's retreats and a staff member of Park Cities Presbyterian Church in Dallas,Texas, relates the story of a state tennis competition in which she participated in high school. She had spent countless hours in practice with her teammates in preparation for the matches. When the tournament rosters were posted, Paige found herself unevenly matched with a young woman named Clara Arnold, who was headed for the professional tennis circuit. Paige was very nervous and realized from the start that she had no hope of victory. She bravely took to the court and was easily defeated, 6-0, 6-0. At the end of a set, she and her opponent were switching courts. She darted over to her coach who was standing on the side of the court and got some water. When she was able to catch her breath enough to speak, she asked him, "Is she playing tennis? Tell me, is she playing tennis?" He said to her, "Yeah honey, that is what we call tennis!" To which she replied, "If that is tennis, then what have I been playing all of this time?"[8] When we are confronted with perfection, we see how very far short we fall.

When we see Jesus face to face, we will be in the presence of perfect righteousness. We will see what it looks like, and we will be fully righteous. When we look at Jesus and see absolute holiness, we will be completely holy. When we gaze at Him and see faultless love, we will be loving. 1 Corinthians 13:12 says, "For now we see in a mirror dimly, but then face to face; now I know in part, but then I shall know fully just as I also have been fully known." A day is coming for believers when His fullness will be revealed and we will be transformed into that image.

So if we are going to be changed by beholding Him, just as He is, when we leave these bodies of flesh, why would we assume that transformation takes place by other means now? We are only changed and transformed now to look like Him and act like Him to the degree that we see

Him as He is now. And this is the ministry of the Holy Spirit in your life. He is seeking to ensure that you are getting a good look at Him and that He is staying "center stage" for the eyes of your heart.

In a sermon on the book of Exodus, Dr. Keller addressed this issue so skillfully that I quote him directly:

> ...of course when we actually see Him fully, face to face, completely apprehending His beauty, we are going to be completely transformed. In fact 1 John 3:1 says, "Beloved, we are children of God and what we will be has not been made known, but we know that when He appears we shall be like Him for we shall see Him as He is." Just seeing Him is going to transform us. But listen to this line, "Everyone who has this hope purifies himself as He is pure." Do you know what that means? That final experience of seeing the glory of God, which is the ultimate thing you were built for, is going to be such a powerful experience that to presently even *hope* for it, to even want it, to even yearn for it, will purify you *now* to some degree.[9]

Beholding changes us, and the ministry of the Holy Spirit is to "glorify" Christ, to let us get a good look at Him.

It is always to our advantage to pray and ask the Father to send the Holy Spirit, to admit our need of Him and our reliance on Him. Luke 11:13-14 says, "If you then, being evil know how to give good gifts to your children, how much more shall your heavenly Father give the Holy Spirit to those who ask Him." The Father longs to send the Spirit and enable us to see Jesus. As a perfect Father He knows how to give us good gifts. He longs for us to ask for the gift of the Spirit.

It is my habit on my weekly day alone with the Lord to head for a window seat at the university library in my hometown. During a recent rendezvous, I got settled, opened my Bible and went to the Lord in prayer. I said something like this, "Father, meet with me. Send the Spirit because I can't even pray without your enabling me." Then I stopped myself and thought, "Oh good grief. I pray for the Father to send the Spirit every week when I come in here. I'll bet God's just up in heaven yawning over the pitiful repetition. He's probably so tired of me praying the same thing week after week." It was then that the Spirit Himself came and reminded me that the Father longs to send me the Spirit. He longs for me to come in humility and ask for His enabling. This is a request that He desires to grant above all.

The Holy Spirit gave me a word picture that helped change my view of constantly asking for the Father to enable me through the Spirit in prayer. The image that I had was that of any one of my three sons coming into my kitchen and saying, "Mom, what can I do to help you?" Since my personal "love language" (the way that I most "feel" loved by others) is "helps," I never, ever get tired of hearing that question. I can't wait to unload some of the numerous tasks needing completion onto willing shoulders. They are asking me for something that I desperately long to give.

Or another way of communicating this concept is to imagine that a teen's parents have come in and asked if the young man would like to have his weekly allowance raised. A teenager never tires of hearing that question, nor does he ever get weary of answering in the affirmative! In the same way, the Father never gets tired of my asking Him to send the Spirit and answering in the affirmative. He can't wait to deliver what He knows I urgently need. He is eager to equip me with the power to remember who I am and get onto my heart the things that are on His heart. He is ever at the ready to have the Spirit turn on the floodlights so Christ gets illuminated for the eyes of my heart to see.

When we forget who we are and move to functionally living in the flesh, the Spirit reminds believers who we really are. Through repentance of deeds of license or legalism and belief in God's promises for us as His children, we are moved back to not only live positionally but also functionally on the right side of the Fork.

Yet the Holy Spirit's ministry is not limited to believers in the world today. He is active in the world at large. He is the restraining factor for evil in general, but He additionally has specific ministry in the lives of those who dwell in the domain of darkness.

So what is the ministry of the Holy Spirit in the life of the non-believer? The Bible tells us that non-believers are spiritually dead. Ephesians 2:1-2 says, "And you were dead in your trespasses and sins in which you formerly walked according to the course of this world...." Non-believers cannot understand spiritual things and have no ability to comprehend truth. They are "natural men" who have no desire to seek God in and of themselves. Because of this condition, non-believers need an outside influence to move in and give them a desire for God, the ability to understand truth and the faith to believe. 1 Corinthians 2:14 says, "But a natural man does not accept the things of the Spirit of God; for they are foolishness to him and he cannot understand them, because they are spiritually appraised." One aspect of the ministry of the Holy Spirit is that He gives insight into spiritual things. He enables the natural man to comprehend things that are spiritually appraised.

In John 16:7-11, Jesus tells us of an additional ministry of the Holy Spirit to non-believers: "But I tell you the truth, it is to your advantage that I go away; for if I do not go away, the Helper shall not come to you; but if I go, I will send Him to you. And He, when He comes, will convict the world concerning sin, and righteousness, and judgment; concerning sin, because they do not believe in Me; and concerning righteousness, because I go to the Father; and you no longer behold Me; and concerning judgment, because the ruler of this world has been judged." Only the Holy Spirit can convince a human heart that it is guilty of breaking the law and the heart of God. Genesis 3:5 says that our hearts are "only evil continually." Apart from the Spirit's intervention, no one seeks after God (Romans 3:11). The Holy Spirit must come in and convict a person of the fact that he does not believe in God nor seek after the things of God. He is like a prosecuting attorney who must secure a verdict of guilty.

In his book on the church, Ed Clowney says this of the Holy Spirit: He is "both attorney and witness; he will convict the world of sin, righteousness and judgment, and he will guide them into all truth (John 16:8,13)."[10] The Spirit is the attorney who must persuade the human heart of sin, yet simultaneously act as a witness "who takes the stand" and speaks the truth of the gospel of grace that will affect the final verdict determined by the heart.   It is His responsibility to show a human heart that it is guilty of living autonomously from God to the degree that the individual is disturbed by the guilt and seeks salvation from it through the truth presented in the Word.

Secondly, the Spirit convicts the non-believer concerning righteousness. John 16 tells us that that He convicts concerning righteousness because "I go to the Father and you no longer behold Me." In this aspect the Spirit is not convincing non-believers *what* righteousness is, but rather *where* righteousness is.   Jesus is true righteousness and He is now at the Father's right hand. Since Jesus' ascension we no longer behold perfect righteousness incarnate, the Word made flesh, but we can know what righteousness is like through the written Word of God. The Spirit convinces us that true righteousness does in fact exist, and He can be received through faith.

Finally, John 16 tells us that the Spirit convicts the non-believer of judgment "because the ruler of this world has been judged." The fact that judgment is real has been demonstrated by the judgment of the ruler of this world, that is Satan. He has already been judged and his power broken at the Cross. In Colossians 2:13-15 Paul is speaking about man's condition apart from Christ and the redemptive work of Christ on the Cross. He mentions the effect of the Cross on the enemies of God when he says, "...having canceled out the certificate of debt consisting of decrees against us and which was hostile to us; and He has taken it out of the way, having nailed it to the cross. When *He had disarmed the rulers and authorities, He made a public display of them, having triumphed over them through Him"* (emphasis mine). At the Cross, Satan was defeated and disarmed.

Non-believers live positionally on the left side of the Fork. They still reside in captivity to the enemy of God. Their entire existence is like a drama enacted in the domain of darkness. All of their behavior is either

82

licentious living or legalistic attempts to attain or maintain a record of righteousness. If they are called and chosen of God, the Holy Spirit intervenes in their lives and they make that initial movement from the domain of darkness into the kingdom of light. It is the cataclysmic movement from the left side of the Fork to the right side that Jesus called being "born again" in John 3. In Colossians 1:13-14 Paul describes it this way: "For He delivered us from the domain of darkness, and transferred us to the kingdom of His beloved Son, in whom we have redemption, the forgiveness of sins." Because of the Cross, man can move from captivity to freedom.

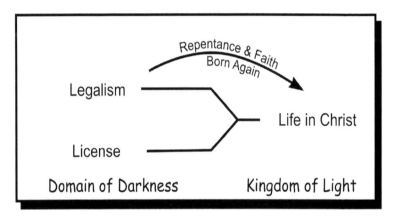

It is only by God's grace that man can make this positional change in residence. God's grace is the cause of man's faith. Ephesians 2:8-9 says, "For by grace you have been saved through faith, and that not of yourselves, it is a gift from God...." His grace is first extended to us. While we were His enemies, He reconciled us to Him through the death of His Son (Romans 5:10). Even the faith to believe in and accept the grace is a gift from Him that is appropriated through the Holy Spirit. On his own, man does not even want God. To even *desire* to live positionally on the right is evidence of the work of the Spirit of God.

Just as we explored how believers can only move from the left side of the Fork to the right through repentance and faith, so too the initial movement from the left side domain of darkness to the right side kingdom of light by non-believers is achieved by repentance and faith. As the Holy Spirit convicts the non-believer of the sin of unbelief in Christ, his heart repents not only of all deeds of unrighteousness, but also of all acts of righteousness motivated from a desire to earn the favor of God or bring something of worth or value other than Christ's perfect righteousness to the Father. For this repentance to result in rightward movement, it must be accompanied by a faith transfer.

Life on the left side of the Fork does not represent a life devoid of faith. All men have faith. We all believe in something at any given moment. Those who are permanent residents in the domain of darkness have placed all of their faith in self. They are self-sufficient. The underlying assumption from which they practically live is that they are adequate in wisdom and resources to run their own lives. It is not that left-side dwellers have no faith, but rather their faith is in falsehoods promoted by the world, the flesh and the devil (Chapter 6). To move from the left to the right side of the Fork does not require the creation of faith, but rather a transfer of it. Faith in self must be replaced by faith in Christ alone.

This faith is not just a generic belief in Jesus, but a belief in the sufficiency of Christ's work on the Cross to provide the blood sacrifice which is required for the turning away of the wrath of God toward sinful man. It is faith that believes there is full and complete forgiveness for sin because Christ's *death* has paid the penalty before the Father for those sins. In addition, this faith understands that Christ's *life of perfect obedience* to the law gets credited to the believer, who as a result has the abiding and abundant love of the Father. When the Spirit works the truth of the necessity of Christ's substitutionary life and death into the minds and hearts of non-believers, they change their permanent address to "Right Side Place."

The kingdom of God on earth is furthered by the work of the Holy Spirit. He causes numerical growth in the church by convincing non-Christians who are living apart from Christ of their need for Him. And He causes organic growth in the church by reminding Christians who have forgotten the life that is theirs in Christ of their ongoing need of Him. The greatest resource the Father has given to the Body for the building of Christ's church is the gift of His Spirit.

Having examined the Holy Spirit on the Fork, let's move on and explore some misconceptions that flow from incomplete or faulty understanding of other Fork concepts. These misunderstandings have serious consequences for the body of Christ. They affect both relationships within the church and the perception of the church by the non-believing world.

Chapter 5
Misconceptions on the Fork

The Fork Illustration is a useful tool for visualizing the truth of the gospel message. Yet it also provides a framework for graphically identifying some pitfalls that we frequently encounter on our spiritual journey. These misconceptions can be divided into conceptual errors and relational errors.

MISCONCEPTION #1
The first conceptual error that we make that can be visually identified on the Fork is our assumption that *repentance* is the movement from the bottom left tine of the Fork up to the top left tine. While Chapter 1 mentions this subtle, yet faulty way of thinking into which we occasionally fall, we will now take time to develop it more fully.

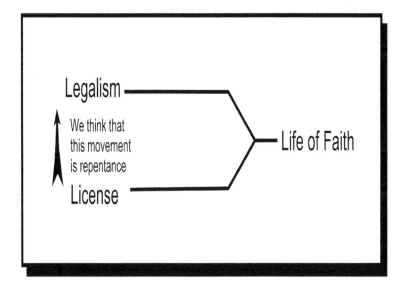

When the Spirit of God convicts us of the sin of rebellious living that disregards the law of God, our desire is for restoration in the relationship we have with our Father. In these moments our natural tendency is to seek restoration though our own efforts and merits. We do this through a variety of self-centered ways. All such efforts are false repentance. So while we naively believe that the movement from the lower left to the upper left tong is true repentance, it is actually a false repentance that will ultimately drive us deeper into our flesh.

One form of false repentance is to want to "clean up our act." These spiritual housekeeping efforts spring from a desire to "do" something about our own sin. In equating repentance with behavior, we confuse true repentance with the fruit or evidences of true repentance. These behavioral attempts at restoration flow from a heart that, at its deepest level, believes God is a demanding Master who insists that we in some way "pay" for our sin.

While it is true that because of His justice, God does require payment for sin, we err in estimating the size of our debt. We mistakenly believe that our debt is manageable and therefore assume we have adequate resources for reimbursement. In reality our debt is of immense proportions. We have committed cosmic treason against the King of the universe and no assets we possess, neither quantitatively nor qualitatively, are sufficient for debt retirement. It is not merely that we do not perform enough good deeds to "balance the scales" against the evil that we do, but our righteous deeds are deficient in their very nature.

According to *Gospel Transformation*, a curriculum developed by World Harvest Mission, "Comparing our righteousness with Christ's righteousness is like comparing apples and oranges. When we endeavor to produce a righteousness of our own, it is as though we are collecting apples. However, the problem is not merely that we acquire only three apples, and God wants us to have a thousand. In reality, God wants oranges, and we have none! We need to understand that Christ's righteousness is quantitatively and qualitatively different from our own."[1] So while God does demand payment for sin, the payment required is of such magnitude and of so foreign a nature to that which man possesses that man must look outside and apart from himself. Only the blood of the perfect Lamb of God, Jesus Christ, is adequate to retire the debt.

Mere acts of rededication and recommitment are misuses of the law which proceed from a mind that is convinced that God keeps us at arms length until **we** can make appropriate restitution for the debt that we owe. These acts will never atone because the very premise upon which they are founded is faulty. And even if we did have the required resources, which we do not, we would not have the resolve to fully make restitution. Our attempts at debt retirement are like "New Year's resolutions." They are commitments that are easily made and easily broken.

While we think that the upward movement is repentance, it is only a façade of true repentance. This upward movement from wrong doing to either right doing or the absence of wrongdoing is the most comfortable course of action to us because it does not require humility or brokenness before a holy God. By atoning for the sin ourselves, our pride remains intact. We are not required to accept anything from anyone for which we were not able to "pay" on our own. Our hearts are so proud that we would rather "do" anything before running to the Cross and acknowledging that we are in desperate need of Christ's atoning work on our behalf, which we can only receive freely. This self-atoning strategy for restitution fails to acknowledge the depth and pervasiveness of our sin. It refuses to see our complete inability to live up to the magnitude of the demands of the law. In this form of false repentance the heart has forgotten that while the Father does indeed require payment for the sin, no matter how much good we do or attempt to do, it will never balance out or cover the magnitude of our sin. In false repentance we also ignore the fact that Christ has already borne the cost for us on the Cross. He has retired the debt that the Father had against us. Because of His sacrifice we are not held at arms length, but can be drawn close to the bosom of our Father in compassion and delight.

A second way that our flesh seeks to atone for the sin of which it is currently experiencing conviction is through penance. One form of penance is contrition, or feeling badly enough about the sin for a long enough time. This technique erroneously assumes that repentance is merely a feeling. The length of time required for the emotional self-abuse usually corresponds to the perceived magnitude of the offense committed. Even in this our reasoning is faulty and we are operating from spiritual blindness. Scripture tells us that sin is sin. No one sin is "bigger" or more wicked than any other. Sin is breaking the heart of God, and lying is just as offensive to Him and wounds Him just as deeply as does murder. The problem with this self-strategy is that while true repentance does involve our emotions, it is not primarily a feeling. In assuming emotional self-abuse to be sufficient payment for sin, we turn our feelings of sorrow over sin into a "work." In essence we are seeking to use that work of "feeling bad" to pay for our sin and restore our fellowship with the Father. Any other inward or outward acts of "penance" from meaningless repetition of memorized prayer to self-flagellation would also fall under this form of false repentance. All such self-abasement is, in essence, self-atonement for sin. Like the first strategy, this second approach also fails to acknowledge we cannot make up for our sin. Only the blood of Christ can wash us clean and restore the sweet communion with our Father.

Merely confession of our sin, intellectual assent and agreement that we have indeed sinned, is also not to be equated with true repentance. We can recognize that we have sinned, spend time evaluating and analyzing the root idolatry behind our sin and even come to the place where we correctly identify the heart motivations driving the fleshly behavior, yet still not truly repent of the sin. Simple cognitive awareness of sin is not equivalent to a broken spirit that is crushed over wounding the heart of our Father. We fail to see that we have committed spiritual adultery and have been unfaithful to the spiritual Lover of our souls, and we neglect to humble ourselves before Him.

Most of us struggle with "besetting" sins. These are areas in our lives where we most easily succumb to temptation. A lack of victory often stems from a lack of repentance. We recognize that once again, we have failed in the same old way. We berate ourselves for our weakness, yet we do not truly repent of the sin before the Father. Were we to consistently repent rather than just analyze and acknowledge, were we to rend our hearts rather than just evaluate them, we would unleash the power of the Holy Spirit and experience victory over these strongholds.

Finally, to assume that repentance is limited to movement from the bottom left tine of the Fork to the top left tine is to presume that we do not need to repent of the legalism or "right doing" in our lives that stems from wrong motivations. The first of Martin Luther's 95 Theses was that all of life is repentance. We are called to repent of our law breaking, but we are also called to repent of our law keeping. Law keeping takes both the form of doing all that the law asks of us and also of refraining from what the law prohibits. On the Fork this can be illustrated as follows:

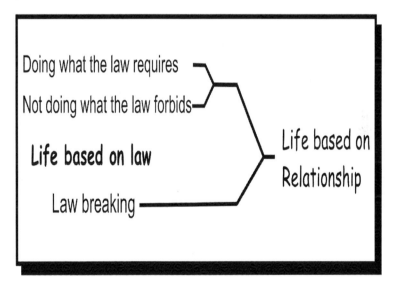

Although we are currently looking at repenting of law keeping in its two forms, just for the sake of thoroughness, let's illustrate that law breaking also has two manifestations.

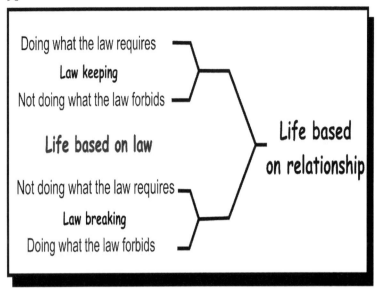

Doing what the law requires

Law keeping

Not doing what the law forbids

Life based on law

Not doing what the law requires

Law breaking

Doing what the law forbids

Life based on relationship

If we believe that repentance is only the movement from license to legalism, we ignore the fact that legalism is also sin. The legalist places his trust in his own work and not that of Christ. His soul is still not at rest in Christ and his confidence is still in self. Habakkuk 2:4 says, "Behold, as for the proud one, *his soul is not right within him;* but the righteous will live by his faith" (emphasis mine).

In the gospel of Matthew, the apostle records how very direct Jesus was in His pronouncements against the Pharisees, the legalists of His day.

> Woe to you, scribes and Pharisees, hypocrites! For you clean the outside of the cup and of the dish, but inside they are full of robbery and self-indulgence. You blind Pharisee, first clean the inside of the cup and of the dish, so that the outside of it may become clean also. Woe to you, scribes and Pharisees, hypocrites! For you are like whitewashed tombs that on the outside appear beautiful, but inside they are full of dead men's bones and all uncleanness. Even so you too outwardly appear righteous to men, but *inwardly you are full of hypocrisy and lawlessness* (Matthew 23:25-28, emphasis mine).

Jesus is saying that cleaning only the outside of the dish or cup - the equivalent of the legalist's attempts to "clean up his act" - still leaves the inside of the cup dirty. And the irony that He exposes is that the lawlessness is *still* within. Legalism cannot eliminate license from our lives.

So what is true repentance and where is it illustrated on the Fork? In the last chapter on the Holy Spirit, we determined that the movement from the left side of the Fork to the right side is accomplished through repentance and faith. True repentance is illustrated on the Fork like this:

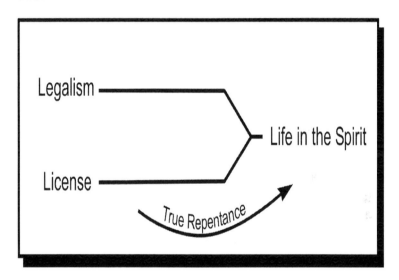

Now that we've spent time examining what false repentance is, what constitutes true repentance? The Puritan writer Thomas Watson outlines six aspects of repentance in his work entitled, *The Doctrine of Repentance*. He says that the first ingredient of true repentance is "sight of sin."[2] By this he means that the Spirit of God must take the Word of God and the law of God and show us that we have fallen short of His standards. As we see the holiness of God reflected in His law, we see how much higher are His ways than our ways and His thoughts than our thoughts (Isaiah 55:9).

Watson goes on to say that the second ingredient for true repentance is sorrow for sin.[3] Self-righteous legalists feel no sorrow over their sin. It does not grieve them nor pierce their hearts. Those who are confident in their own ability to bring some form of goodness to God with which to recommend themselves do not mourn over their sin. The self-righteous fail to grieve over sin in part because they do not even see it. In his book, *Love Walked Among Us*, Paul Miller likens self-righteousness to bad breath. He says, "A bad hair day is just that; a bad hair day. Everyone sees it, including you. But bad breath is different. Others smell it, but you can't. Self-righteousness...is like bad breath. Others can smell it, but you can't."[4] In most cases, we are unaware of our self-righteousness. Spiritual blindness prevents acknowledgment and distress over our sin.

Thomas Watson continues to unfold the meaning of true repentance for us by claiming that the third aspect is a matter of confessing our sin.[5] When we confess sin we must be specific in the confession and we must absolve God from all blame. Acts of renewal should be as specific as the acts of rebellion. We need to name the offense and acknowledge exactly how we have sought to live autonomously from the Father. We personally own the sin and lay the blame at our door. We need to come to the place where we can say as the prophet Nehemiah, "However, Thou art just in all that has come upon us; for Thou hast dealt faithfully, but we have acted wickedly" (Nehemiah 9:33). We must be willing to remove any implication of wrong doing from God or others.

The fourth component of repentance listed by Watson is shame for sin.[6] He states, "Blushing is the color of virtue. When the heart has been made black with sin, grace makes the face red with blushing...."[7] In our modern culture shame is virtually an unknown quality. The degree to which relativism has overtaken modern thought is proportionate to the disappearance of shame in our society. Relativism is the belief that all value systems are equally true. Those who adhere to this philosophy believe that right and wrong are determined at an individual level. The relativist says that truth is based on personal convictions and exists in as many varieties as there are individuals. Relativism insists that there are no moral absolutes. Within a system of such moral fluidity, because there are no standards, there can be no violations of standards. If no infringement of a given standard has occurred, then there is no opportunity for guilt. If there is no guilt, then there is no associated shame. The more our society adheres to relativism, the less its members acknowledge the existence of shame.

The problem with this theoretical framework is that most who subscribe to it do not live consistently with their view. While relativists may claim to believe there is no objective standard for moral behavior, most do believe, for example, that murder, rape or racial discrimination is wrong. Because they cannot remove the innate sense of right and wrong, while they may not outwardly acknowledge guilt and its corresponding shame, it nonetheless exists within them and torments them on a subconscious level.

Webster's Dictionary defines shame as "a painful feeling of having lost the respect of others because of improper behavior or incompetence; dishonor or disgrace."[8] In *When People Are Big and God Is Small*, Edward Welch says that those who are experiencing shame feel "exposed, vulnerable and in desperate need of covering or protection."[9] When we are ashamed of our sin we feel disgrace, separate from grace and we recognize our desperate need of covering or protection. Thomas Watson displays great insight when he includes this as a vital part of true repentance.

The fifth characteristic of repentance, according to Watson, is hatred for sin.[10] Watson writes that "Christ is never loved till sin be loathed. Heaven is never longed for till sin be loathed...Let all my self-love be turned into self-loathing (Zechariah 3:4-5). We are never more precious in God's eyes than when we are lepers in our own."[11] Do we really hate sin? Are we as passionate in our abhorrence of it as we are in our devotion to our idols? Scripture tells us that the fear of the Lord is to hate evil (Proverbs 8:13).

Finally, the sixth aspect listed by Watson is turning from sin.[12] This last category, the turning from the sin, is what we most commonly assume repentance to be. While producing fruit in keeping with repentance is one aspect of repentance, it is not the whole of it. The behaviors which flow out of true repentance are important and serve as a gauge as to whether repentance has indeed taken place, but they are not the repentance itself. To attempt to reduce repentance to this one aspect is to lose it in its entirety. Either these characteristics of repentance are all present or repentance is not present at all.

Distinguishing false repentance from true repentance can be quite tricky on the surface; that is, outwardly, the two can look exactly the same. Those who call in the spiritual housekeeper and merely move from the bottom left tine to the top left one can produce deeds that mirror the fruit of true repentance. Only God can know for sure the actual motivation for the outward manifestations. While our vision is limited to the outward appearance, God discerns the heart. And true repentance can ultimately only be perceived at a heart level. In addition, false repentance will not produce long-term change. Because it is not real change occurring at a heart level, it will not be durable. The next time the individual is confronted with a similar temptation, a return to license will most likely result.

True repentance is a despairing of any righteousness of our own. It is a broken and humbled heart that recognizes that it never had and never will have anything of its own to bring to God except sin. Rick Downs, a pastor in the Presbyterian Church of America, provides this definition for repentance: "Repentance is a matter of coming before God Himself, seeing our sin and rejoicing in the gospel. Change (that is, the fruit in keeping with repentance) becomes almost an activity that we observe rather than an activity we perform."[13]

MISCONCEPTION #2

Not only do we mistakenly believe that repentance is movement from the bottom left tine to the top left tine, we make the corresponding conceptual error in the assumption that *sin* is moving from the top left tine to the bottom left tine.

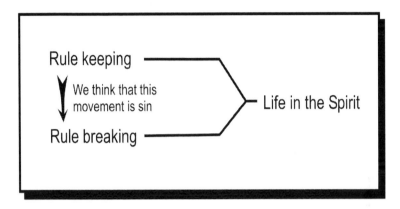

To view sin simply as law breaking is to have an anemic definition of sin. The Bible gives us a much richer and fuller understanding of sin. The story of a foreign female infant who has been abandoned is recounted in Ezekiel 16.

> Then the word of the Lord came to me saying, "Son of man, make known to Jerusalem her abominations, and say, 'Thus says the Lord God to Jerusalem, "Your origin and your birth are from the land of the Canaanite, your father was an Amorite and your mother a Hittite. As for your birth, on the day you were born your navel cord was not cut, nor were you washed with water for cleansing; you were not rubbed with salt or even wrapped in cloths. No eye looked with pity on you to do any of these things for you, to have compassion on you. Rather you were thrown out into the open field, for you were abhorred on the day you were born. When I passed by you and saw you squirming in your blood, I said to you while you were in your blood, 'Live!' I made you numerous like plants of the field. Then you grew up, became tall, and reached the age for fine ornaments; your breasts were formed and you hair had grown. Yet you were naked and bare. Then I passed by you and saw you, and behold, you were at the time for love; so I spread My skirt over you and covered your nakedness. I also swore to you and entered into a covenant with you so that you became Mine," declares the Lord. "Then I bathed you with water, washed off your blood from you and anointed you with

oil. I also clothed you with embroidered cloth, and put sandals of porpoise skin on your feet; and I wrapped you with fine linen and covered you with silk. And I adorned you with gold and silver, and your dress was of fine linen, silk, and embroidered cloth. You ate fine flour, honey and oil; so you were exceedingly beautiful and advanced to royalty. Then your fame went forth among the nations on account of your beauty, for it was perfect because of My splendor which I bestowed on you," declares the Lord. "But you trusted in your beauty and played the harlot because of your fame, and you poured out your harlotries on every passer-by who might be willing...And besides all your abominations and harlotries you did not remember the days of your youth, when you were naked and bare and squirming in your blood. Then it came about after all your wickedness ('Woe, woe to you!' declares the Lord God), that you built yourself a shrine and made yourself a high place in every square. You built yourself a high place at the top of every street, and made your beauty abominable; and you spread your legs to every passer-by to multiply your harlotry." ' "

The infant in this passage represents Israel, and the Lord is depicted as the savior who rescues her. Without His intervention she would have surely died in the wilderness where she was forsaken. The Lord says that He passed by and said to her, "Live!" He took her into his own home and raised her. He made provision for her and fully bore the cost for her every need. She grew and reached an age for "fine ornaments." He protected her and generously met her needs until she was "at the time for love." Then the Lord does an amazing thing. He takes this woman who has no family, no dowry and nothing of her own that did not come directly from Him and He marries her. He enters into a covenant with her. When the text says that she "became His," Ezekiel means that she became his wife. He adorns her with jewels and fine clothing and her fame goes out among the nations. Then in verse 15 we are told that she trusted in her beauty and plays the harlot. She offers favors to "every passer-by who might be willing." She becomes a prostitute and sells herself on every street corner. In this passage, Scripture does not give us a definition of sin, but a rather a very graphic metaphor of sin. The description goes far beyond the phraseology of a simple definition. God wants us to get a vivid picture of the essence of sin. Sin is spiritual adultery. It is taking the affection, compassion and generosity of the Lover of our soul and throwing it in His face. We, like the woman of Ezekiel 16, do not simply stray once, learn our lesson, and then return. Spiritually speaking, we routinely practice our harlotry on every street corner. When we sin, we give our love, affection, adoration and worship to something other than God and we do it in two ways.

First of all, we sin by law breaking. We indulge our flesh in an attempt to find the love and acceptance that only comes from Him. We worship and serve things that are not God, thinking that they can give us the significance and peace we desire. These things increasingly demand more to be satisfied and ultimately enslave us. The one thing idols never say to us is "enough." We can never quench their thirst, and the quest to satiate them exhausts us and leaves us frustrated, burned out and despondent. Thousands of Americans, even American Christians, feel over extended and overwhelmed because of the endless demands of our idols. Jesus tells us that His yoke is easy and His burden is light. "Easy" and "light" are not the first words that come to mind when most of us are asked to describe our lives. Americans adhere to the McDonald's philosophy of life, believing that they "deserve a break today." "Actually, we do need a break today. Our idols leave us exhausted and empty with no energy left for love."[13] While idols can be temporarily gratified, they are never permanently satisfied. The break that we need can only come from the message of cessation of work unto righteousness that is heralded in the gospel.

All sin, or spiritual adultery, is idolatry. An obvious illustration of the enslavement that comes from idolatry is seen in a man who indulges the flesh by using marijuana. The demands of his flesh are never silenced, never satiated. One high is not enough. He begins to live for the next joint he can obtain. Soon, marijuana is not enough, so he moves on to crack. His life becomes an endless pursuit of a new and more intense high. Initially, funding a drug addiction is manageable. But as the addiction cycle intensifies, to support drug use, addicts are often driven to illegal means to sustain their habit. As the frequency of drug use and the cost of the drugs increase, in many instances, so too does the criminal activity. The user is now enslaved by an addiction. It consumes his whole being and is the focus of his entire existence. His addiction is practiced on "on every street corner" and his search for meaning apart from God is analogous to spiritually harlotry with lover gods. Sin is idolatry, and that idolatry is addictive.

But while we commit spiritual adultery through law breaking, we also evidence our harlotry through law keeping. Giving ourselves to things that are "good" in the hope of attaining the love and acceptance we crave is also spiritual adultery. We so easily take desires for things that are good and turn them into over desires. Things that God created and gave to us as gifts, things which usually have positive, God-given purposes, are twisted by our flesh and become things that we *must* have. A simple example of this is the man who works diligently to support his family. Adequate financial provision is a good thing for him to pursue. It is God honoring and necessary to provide materially for the family with which God has blessed him. Yet if he cannot rest easily without a certain dollar amount in his investment portfolio, it could be that it has become a false god. If he spends 60 hours a week at work and ignores his own spiritual and physical needs and those of his family, then he may need to examine his heart to determine if he has climbed into bed with the god of financial security. When we settle for the fulfillment of these desires as ends in themselves rather than as means to the end of experiencing God as the ultimate fulfillment of every desire, we short change ourselves. We settle for far too little when the majesty, beauty, splendor, love and graciousness of the Creator is available.

To assume that sin is simply moving from the upper left tine of the Fork to the lower left tine is not merely a far too narrow view of sin; it is an erroneous one. Sin is the movement from the right *side*, to the left *side* of the Fork. It is illustrated as follows:

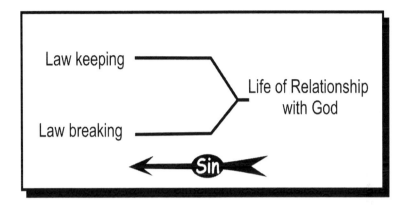

Romans 14:23 tells us that *whatever* is not of faith is sin. Neither law breaking nor law keeping requires faith in Christ. As such, both are equally sinful.

The third and fourth errors that we can see illustrated on the Fork are relational errors. Dividing walls are erected both within personal relationships and within the church when we fall into either of these fallacies. They are both the result of either having forgotten who we are in Christ or not ever having understood the gospel at all.

MISCONCEPTION #3

Error number three occurs when a person who is either living functionally or positionally as a legalist looks at a person who is abiding on the right side of the Fork. In essence, it is a rule keeping orphan looking at someone who is living in freedom as a son or daughter of God. The legalist knows only law as the basis for relating to God. He or she must do all the law requires or refrain from all the law forbids. The practical Pharisee is enslaved to law, and rules are central to all of life. Misconception #3 occurs when the legalist looks at someone who lives free from "rule keeping for righteousness," due to his or her identity in Christ, and says, "Antinomian! You don't love the law of

God! You abuse the grace of God! You are licentious!"
On the Fork, this can be visualized as follows:

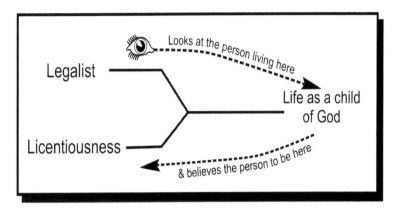

Looks at the person living here

Legalist

Life as a child
of God

Licentiousness

& believes the person to be here

While there may indeed be a problem with the person
living in freedom, the legalist cannot know that for sure
simply on the basis of outward appearances. Only God
can see the heart. Only He can determine if the behavior
of His child is born of freedom or license.

Judging one another springs from a lack of assurance
that we are His and fully loved. Irrespective of whether the
legalism is functional or positional, a person living as a
legalist must judge others to gain or maintain superiority
and security. Legalistic hearts do not understand freedom
as a proper motivation behind a believer's behavior. The
legalist looks at the liberty of a Christian who knows the
love of God and says, "This person is not really even a
Christian. He does not obey the law like I do. If he was a
'real' Christian, like me, he would not live that way!"

A practical example of this error in thinking could be
the issue of attending movies. Some hold incredibly strong
convictions that movie going is sin, and for that person
attending a movie would be. But for this "non-movie goer"
to look at a Christian brother who feels the freedom in
Christ to attend a movie and condemn him is judgmental.
The one who is refraining from movie attendance cannot
see the heart of his brother. To automatically assume that
the movie attendee is licentious in his action is in itself

sinful and is part of why we have divisions within our churches.

MISCONCEPTION #4

This final error in thinking is also a relational one. This error is made by a person who is either functionally or positionally living on the bottom left tine of the Fork, that is, living licentiously. Believers still have the capacity to sin. So, although we positionally live on the right side of the Fork, we move functionally to the left. When a person who is living in rebellion looks at a Christian he sees a saint who sins.

The licentious non-Christian does not believe or understand what living out of the gospel of grace looks like at all. This individual tends to view the person who identifies himself with Christ yet still sins with suspicion. The sinful saint is perceived by the morally rebellious as a hypocrite because, in general, the licentious individual believes that moral reformation or using the law for justification is equivalent to salvation or sanctification. He is convinced that "good living" is all that God requires. If this is what he thinks being spiritual is all about, when someone claims to be a Christian and yet falls into sin, in the eyes of the licentious he is just a hypocrite, a Pharisee who wants to put others under law yet can't even keep law himself. For example, suppose a non-Christian is driving down the road and a car pulls out in front of him, cutting him off in traffic and forcing him to brake sharply. The non-Christian is so close to the bumper of the offending car that he could practically kiss the *icthus* (Christian "fish" symbol) that is attached to the rear of the vehicle. He thinks to himself, "See, that's one of those Christians! They're supposed to be good. They believe in 'Do unto others as you would have them do unto you.' What a bunch of hypocrites! They're no different from me but they think they're better." This attitude demonstrates that the non-Christian does not understand that true believers do not feel they are better than others, but in reality, they see the depth and scope of their sin and feel that they are, in fact, worse. Yet at the same time, Christians know they are deeply loved and accepted and are assured of future glory. Because of a faulty view of what Biblical Christianity is, the non-Christian looks at the believer, judges him and finds him lacking on the basis of his own misconceptions. On the basis of the faulty assumption that Christianity and morality are one in the same, the non-believer misjudges the believer. When the assumptions behind our reasoning are faulty, the resulting conclusions will also be erroneous.

Not only do we see non-Christians living licentiously, but believers can also functionally live on the bottom left side of the Fork. The Christian who is living licentiously has forgotten what he knows. His flesh has chosen to believe the lies of the world and the accusations of the devil and the result is rebellious behaviors that are in contrast to the law of God. He can develop a judgmental spirit that flows from his current spiritual blindness. For example, a young man within the church who professes Christ has sexual sin exposed. Let's suppose that the elders of the congregation confront him in love. Their goal is restoration of this brother. And let's assume that the confrontation is done in a Biblical, caring manner. Now, this brother can repent and believe as he is reminded of the truth of the gospel or he can seek to avoid acknowledgment of his sin by blame shifting. In this case, when confronted he might reason to himself, "What right do these men have to speak into my life? They are just a bunch of sinners like me. Why, just last week I heard Joe speak harshly to his wife. And yesterday when Bob gave me a ride over to the auto parts store I saw how he looked at the scantily clad jogger as we passed by. These guys are no different from me. In fact, I'm better than they are because at least I am not hiding my sin nor do I speak to people in the same manner as Joe did. What a bunch of white washed tombs! I don't have to listen to them."

For those who have forgotten who they are in Christ confrontation is threatening. In the face of exposed sin they tend to 1) criticize those who confront them, 2) blame shift by scrutinizing the life of the confronter and identifying how he commits the same sin, although perhaps to a lesser or greater degree, and 3) judge the confronter as judgmental himself. All of these responses are part of a subconscious strategy for self-justification and serve to avoid repentance and restoration.

Underlying this man's attitude is the idea that if he can put others down he can somehow elevate himself and salvage pride. His heart is hardened and he refuses to humble himself. He has forgotten that there is grace for repentant sinners. He looks at the elders, saints who are still sinners, and uses their failings to justify his own sin. He self-righteously judges his fellow believers. He finds and condemns them as sinners and hypocrites. Are these men sinful? Yes, and if they are operating out of their identity in Christ they are quick to acknowledge that fact. The difference between them and the man is that they can admit their sin because they know that there is grace for the humble sinner who comes to Christ in need. When believers forget the gospel and turn to licentiousness, a common result is judgmental attitudes, condemnation and division within the church.

This is illustrated on the Fork as follows:

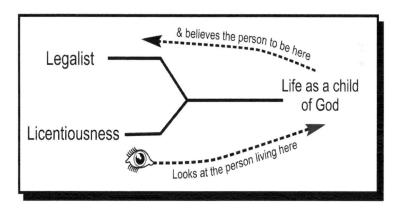

It is only when the licentious, whether believer or non-believer, come to understand the message of the gospel of grace that they are enabled to forsake judgmental attitudes toward others. The gospel of grace says that Christians are simultaneously saints and sinners. We are guilty before a holy God, yet we are justified and legally declared righteous in Christ. Only through the Cross can a person be, at once, a saint and a sinner. And only those who understand that Christians are both totally depraved and totally loved at the same time are able to avoid this fourth misconception.

The work of the Body of Christ is seriously hindered when misconceptions #3 and #4 are left unaddressed. Factions, hatred, condemnation of fellow believers and church splits are possible consequences of these failures to understand the gospel. The application of truth through the public and private proclamation of the Word of God is the sole solution. The Spirit of God must take the Word of God and penetrate hearts with the good news of the gospel of grace.

We now have a working knowledge of the Fork Illustration and the concepts that it depicts. We have also looked at possible errors that result from a lack of understanding of the gospel's application to life after conversion. In the remaining chapters we will go on to expand the diagram to include the enemies and resources that we have in the Christian life.

Chapter 6
The Enemies of the Believer on the Fork

Thus far we have seen only one of the enemies of the Christian illustrated on the Fork. In Chapter One, we saw that the Fork Illustration contrasts life in the "flesh" with life in the Spirit. But the flesh is not our only enemy.

Ephesians 2:1-3 specifically lists three enemies that fight together against believers. Paul says,

> And you were dead in your trespasses and sins, in which you formerly walked according to *the course of this world*, according to the *prince of the power of the air*, of the spirit that is now working in the sons of disobedience. Among them we too all formerly lived in the *lusts of our flesh*, indulging the desires of the flesh and of the mind, and were by nature children of wrath, even as the rest (emphasis added).

In life, believers battle against the world, the flesh and the devil. These three enemies form an alliance and work conjunctively to render a Christian ineffective and joyless. The world, the flesh and the devil are a coalition of enemies. Say, for example, that the United States was at war. If our country was being attacked from the west by Russia, from the east by England and from the south by Mexico this would be a picture of us fighting against three enemies. But if we were being attacked from the west, east and south by combined forces from Russia, England and Mexico that would be a war against a coalition. The world, flesh and devil work together and simultaneously wage war on various fronts in our lives.

Before a person becomes a Christian, he has one enemy, God. Romans 5:10 says, "For if while we were enemies, we were reconciled to God through the death of His Son, much more having been reconciled, we shall be saved by His life." But when a person puts his faith and trust in Jesus Christ's sacrificial work on the Cross for salvation, he is granted peace with God. Romans 5:1 says, "Therefore having been justified by faith, we have peace with God through our Lord Jesus Christ." The wrath of God (John 3:36) no longer abides on him and he is transferred from the domain of darkness into the kingdom of light. Although one benefit of this relocation is peace with God, one ramification is that His enemies now become our enemies. The enemies of the world, the flesh and the devil are out to destroy us.

THE FLESH

The flesh with its two faces has already been illustrated for us on the Fork. When talking about the flesh, we are not referring to our "skin." In Scripture man is divided into two distinct parts, body and spirit. The body deals with the physical aspect of our being. Our epidermis, our bones, our organs and tissues, our circulatory and respiratory systems are all parts of our physical body. Scripture also speaks of our spirit or soul. The Bible also uses the term "heart" to describe this non-physical part of us.

The soul/spirit can be broken down to our mind, will and affections. These three parts of us work together just like our heart, lungs and brain. They are interdependent and each is necessary for life. If any one of the three malfunctions or is removed, death is imminent.

This can be depicted as follows:

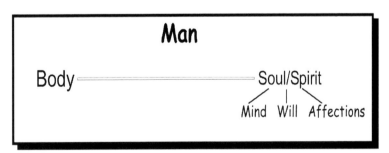

The mind is that part of us where we reason, doubt, think, remember, and discern. It is the seat of our beliefs, understandings, memories and judgments. It is the intellectual part of us.

The term "affections" is an old Puritan word that includes our emotions, but encompasses so much more. Our affections are comprised of our emotions, feelings, longings, desires and imaginings. In her wonderful book, *Idols of the Heart*, Elyse Fitzpatrick says this about our emotions:

> ...emotions are mirrors of our hearts. Our emotions reveal our thoughts and intentions, they reveal the judgments we've made about our circumstances. Our fears, sorrows, or joys are the ways we vividly experience the results of our thoughts and desires. If you are experiencing a particular emotion, that's usually because you've harbored certain thoughts or desires in your heart that give rise to this feeling. For instance, if you feel sad, it's usually because your thoughts or desires have been disappointed in some way. Your responses to the trials or blessings of life are the primary causes of the emotions you feel daily. If you feel like jumping for joy, again that's due to the fact that your thoughts and desires are pleased. Our feelings work in concert with our affections, our minds, our wills and our consciences.[1]

The will is that part of us that chooses or determines our actions. The will is informed by our mind and affections about the best course of action and then the will executes it.

Our flesh is made up of the mind, will and affections. The "flesh" is that part of us that desires above all to live lives independent of God. Alternate phraseology for living in the flesh is being self-sufficient. It is the part of us that yearns for autonomy and aspires to actually *be* God.

We saw this visually represented on the Fork this way:

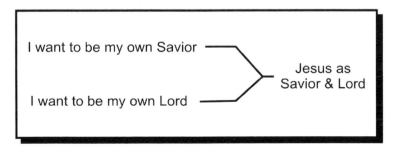

THE WORLD

Now we move to the second member of the Christian's adversarial coalition, the world.

> The Bible's use of the term "world" is not simple. As God made it and keeps it, the world is good. God pronounced it very good at the time of creation, and He promises the restoration of a new heaven and earth. As a rebellious world, however, it is bad. The people of the world have become God's enemies. The world became the domain of the devil.... Yet the world, as a lost world, is both doomed and spared. It is doomed by God's judgment against it. It is spared, however, in God's longsuffering mercy, and it is made the object of God's love.... This fallen, broken world is now Christ's world. It is the theater of His redemption, the place of His mission....[2]

When New Testament writers talk about the world, various words are used. One, *oikoumene,* means the inhabited earth. It speaks of the spherical shaped object revolving around the sun upon which we live. A second word which we translate world is *kosmos,* which means order or system. This use of the word "world" can represent a mindset or grid through which we interpret all of life. When we speak of the "world" as an enemy of the believer, it is in this context. The world is a belief system that tells us how to understand reality.

How are we influenced by the world and its thinking? Daily we are bombarded with advertisements on our televisions. We are told everything from how we should look and what we should drive to what we need to serve on our tables and rub under our armpits to "be somebody." Newspapers and now the Internet news websites influence the formation of our opinions about right and wrong, how to invest our resources and how to live our lives. Magazines affect our decisions on what to wear, how to style our hair, which brand of make-up to use and how to solve our relational problems. We are surrounded by worldly thinking. In short, the world tells us what we need to be "OK," to matter, to fit in or be significant. The world can be drawn on the Fork illustration as follows:

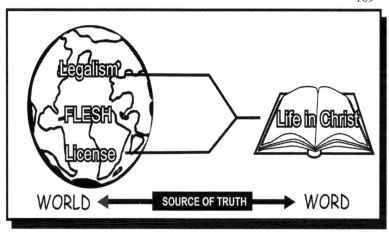

In direct contrast to the lies of the world stands the Word of God. All humans choose which source they look to for truth. Scripture warns us against the dangers of the world. 1 John 2:15-16 says, "Do not love the world, nor the things in the world. If anyone loves the world, the love of the Father is not in him. For all that is in the world, the lust of the flesh, the lust of the eyes and the boastful pride of life is not from the Father, but is from the world."

The lust of the flesh refers to our desire to satisfy our physical desires. These are the cravings we have for food, sex, rest and drink. While these are good, God-given desires, our flesh grabs on to what the world suggests that we need and demands that we obtain it. Our desires for good things become ultimate and therefore take the place in our lives that God says rightfully belongs to Him alone. Paul encourages us in Romans 13:14, "But put on the Lord Jesus Christ and make no provision for the flesh in regard to its lusts."

The lust of the eyes includes those desires within us for material things. Again, where God has given us healthy desires for comfort and beauty, which were to point us to Him for their fulfillment, our flesh turns these longings into over desires that produce all sorts of rotten fruit in our lives. In Matthew 6:33 Jesus bids us to "Seek first His kingdom and His righteousness; and all these things shall be added to you."

And finally the pride of life speaks of that desire within us to have the universe revolve around "self." It is the yearning of our hearts to be self-sufficient, self-ruling, self-atoning and independent of any alternate authority. This self-exaltation is idolatry. We are commanded in Exodus 20:1-3, "Then God spoke all these words, saying, 'I am the Lord your God, who brought you out of the land of Egypt, out of the house of slavery. You shall have no other gods before Me.'" The pride of life puts "self" in the place of God.

Scripture warns us that the lust of the flesh, the lust of the eyes and the pride of life constitute worldliness. World Harvest Mission's course, Gospel Transformation, says that the chief characteristic of worldliness is boasting.[3] We tend to think of boasting as bragging about things which have done or are able to do well. Boasting is much more than this. Boasting is an all-consuming concentration on self. We are never so boring to others as when we boast. Boasting is the commonality for all man. Not all sin in the same way, so we can't define worldliness in light of any given sin, but rather as boasting: "...What we love to talk about indicates what we boast in. That is why we talk so much about ourselves."[4]

Worldliness is only overcome at the Cross. The Apostle Paul stated this when he penned Galatians 6:14: "But may it never be that I should boast, except in the cross of our Lord Jesus Christ, through which the world has been crucified to me and I to the world." Here Paul claims that boasting in the Cross is contrary to a worldly mindset.

THE DEVIL

The third enemy in the coalition of adversaries of the believer is the devil. While the word Satan means "enemy," the word devil means "accuser." Whether we call him Satan or the devil, Scripture tells us that he is a liar and the father of lies. He is introduced to us in Genesis 3, where we find him slandering God to Eve. Satan asks Eve, "Has God said?" Satan is not all-powerful, nor omnipotent, as God is. He is not all knowing, nor omniscient, as God is. Neither can he be in more than one place at any given time. He is not omnipresent as God is. There are practical implications to all of these characteristics revealed in Scripture about the devil. If we are believers, the stronghold that Satan once had in our lives has been broken. "Greater is He who is in you than he who is in the world" (1 John 4:4).

While the devil cannot cause a believer to lose his salvation, that is, to move *positionally* from the right side of the Fork to the left, he can influence you to move there *functionally*. His goal is to cause believers to forget who we are, to lose our joy and to live functionally as orphans.

If, as we saw in Chapter 4, the *ministry* of the Holy Spirit is to **influence** us to move from the left side of the Fork to the right through repentance and faith, then the *mission* of the Devil is to **incite** us to functionally move from the right side to the left, to life in the flesh, through boasting and unbelief. We see this depicted on the Fork:

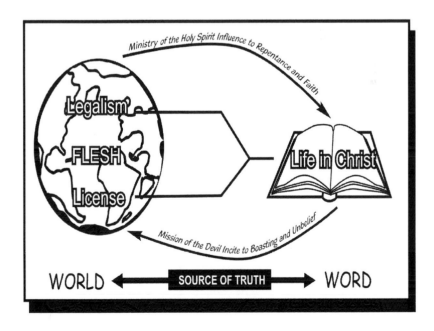

　　If you remember, we said in Chapter 4 that the Holy Spirit's ministry is to remind us of who we are in Christ. He brings to mind the things of Christ and all that we have in Him. He tells us that we *are* rich and that we *are* somebody special, we belong to and are loved by the King. Everything is ours. Contrarily, the devil's mission is to whisper to us that we *are* nothing and *have* nothing. His primary message to us is that God is a miser who is holding out on us. As the consummate deceiver, his goal is to incite us to believe any of his multitudinous lies about the true character of God. In his book, *Addictions: A Banquet in the Grave*, Edward Welch says this of believers: "You believe lies about God. Guaranteed. You think he can't see all things; you think he doesn't care; you think that he reluctantly forgives; you think that he is far away; you think that he loves many people but not you."[5] All of these falsehoods are flames ignited by the world and fanned by the covert murmurings of the devil. His strategy is not new. This is the same tactic that he used with Eve in the Garden. Genesis 3: 4-5 says, "And the serpent said to the woman, 'You surely shall not die! For God knows that in the day you eat from it your eyes will be opened, and you will be like God, knowing good and evil.'" Satan subtly implies that "there is more," that Adam and Eve could "be" more and "have" more. The logical conclusion to which he attempts to lead Eve is that God is holding out on her.

　　1 Corinthians 2:12 says, "Now we have received, not the spirit of the world, but the Spirit who is from God, ***that we might know the things feely given to us by God.***" The Spirit reminds us that the Father has given us everything in Christ, freely. Just as the Spirit of God takes the truths of the Word about who we are in Christ and **applies** them to our hearts, so, too, Satan takes the lies of the world and **articulates** them to our hearts. He says to us, "You have nothing. He will give you nothing but pain and suffering. If He blesses you at all, He only does so sparingly and stingily. Go out there and get those things for yourself. You need them! You are nothing without them!" The Spirit reminds us from Romans 8:32 that "He who did not spare His own Son, but delivered Him up for

us all, how will He not also with Him freely give us all things?" He willingly provided His own Son for us. Scripture plainly tells us that He has not even withheld that which is most precious to Him, Jesus. He is definitely not holding out on us.

THE COALITION

So how do these three enemies work together? Our flesh latches on to the lies that the world and the devil propagate. When the world and the devil tell us that we need certain things to be significant and to matter, our flesh not only desires those things, but craves them to the point of obsession. The flesh must obtain those things to be content, or find meaning and purpose.

In her book, *Idols of the Heart*, Elyse Fitzpatrick puts it this way:

> The devil's temptation occurs in our hearts in concert with the influences of the world and our fleshly natures. The lies of the world and our deceitful thoughts and desires are useful tools in his attack. Satan uses two powerful weapons in this attack: fear and pleasure. He tempts us through fear by suggesting that obedience to God will result in the loss of something we believe we must have in order to be happy. At the same time he tempts us through pleasure by portraying the joys that disobedience will bring us. His temptation does not put anything into us that is not there already. We succumb to Satan's temptations because of the lusts that already live in our hearts.[6]

Again, Dr. Timothy Keller provides a helpful illustration. He explains that Satan and his demons are like musicians, but not singers. Satan and his minions need instruments to play. They cannot make any music without the aid of a piano or violin or flute. They must have something with which to work. Our flesh is that instrument in us through which they work. Dr. Keller quotes a man named John White, who claims that if you lift up the top of a piano and sing a note into it, all of the strings will remain motionless except for the string that matches the note that you sang. That string will vibrate and you will hear an echo because there is something in that string which resonates with your voice.[7] The point is that Satan needs footholds in our lives, things with which he can resonate. These footholds are found in our characteristic flesh.

The following is just a sampling of questions that might be used to identify our characteristic flesh.[8]

- What must I have in my life to be "OK?"
- What do I most fear?
- What do I most desire?
- Whose opinion of me matters most?
- What, if I lost it, would make me feel that life was no longer worth living?
- On what do I spend significant amounts of money?
- To what do I devote my time?
- What really matters to me?
- Who can make it all better?
- What would make me feel secure?
- What do I think about most often? What do I obsess over?
- What, if I had it, would make everything all right?
- What most irritates me?

Knowing the answers to these questions can aid in our preparation for combat against the attacks of the coalition. Properly identifying our characteristic flesh can allow us to be better equipped to hear when the enemy sounds our particular "notes," and to call upon the Spirit to effectively still the strings within our hearts.

Elyse Fitzpatrick gives a scriptural example of this phenomenon by citing the temptation of Judas.

> When Satan tempted Judas, he was successful because it was in Judas's character to love money. Judas was already an idolater. He loved money more than he loved the Lord, so it wasn't much of a stretch to betray Jesus for thirty pieces of silver. Judas was easy prey for Satan's attack because his love for the Lord was overshadowed by his love for the prestige and respect that money brings...his idolatry turned out to be the snare that brought his ultimate destruction. Satan planted fear in his heart that Christ would never oust the Romans while at the same time enticing him with the thoughts of the pleasure that thirty pieces of silver would bring.[9]

When she mentions that the love of money was the "snare" that brought ultimate destruction to Judas, Elyse Fitzpatrick is saying that this was the piano "string" in his life upon which Satan found resonance.

Here we see one of the implications for Satan's lack of omniscience. Because Satan is not all knowing, he does not know which areas are our weakest. It is not that he knows all and can effectively go straight for the "chinks" in our armor. So how then does he know how to effectively tempt us? The answer is that he does not. Satan and his demons constantly sing demonic scales of temptation into the piano of our lives. We only notice the temptation, or resonance, when they happen to "sound" our characteristic flesh. For example, my yard can be a disaster. There can be dandelions and crab grass scattered all over the Bermuda 419 that my husband so carefully tends. I don't lose a single moment of sleep over this. Frankly, I don't even notice it. But, should one of my sons come racing through the back door after having tromped through the mud and leave dirty footprints all over my recently cleaned kitchen floor, I go ballistic. The appearance of the yard is not an idol for me, but a clean kitchen floor is. Satan or his minions sound the note of yard weeds in my life, but it has nothing with which to resonate. Yet, when the chord of filthy linoleum is struck, the vibrations are of seismic proportion!

WHO IS THE CULPRIT?

Christians wander into a minefield when we spend excessive amounts of time and energy attempting to determine which of these three enemies is the source of our current problems. The unholy trinity of the world, the flesh and the devil works together, and all three are usually involved in some capacity. When we seek to target and battle on one front alone, we usually fall into error.

If we were to assume that the world, a wrong mindset, is the villain to the exclusion of the flesh and the devil, we erroneously conclude that right thinking will be the solution to our problems. We begin to focus on doctrine. Our theology must be right. Our doctrine must be pure. And while right doctrine is not bad or evil in itself, when it becomes our focus and obsession, we mutate into Pharisees who have heads full of right thinking and hearts full of self-righteousness at how much we know. We just move from one area of sin or temptation into another one and are no better off.

If we focus our assault on the devil and assume that he is the primary culprit, we can become consumed with the supernatural. We see the devil or his demons in everything "bad" that happens to us from hang nails to church splits. The pervasive theme of our prayer life becomes "binding and casting out," and we assume a spiritually defensive posture. We lose sight of the magnitude of our "flesh" problem and fail to deal with the sin and idolatry in our own hearts.

And, finally, if we lay all of the blame on the doorstep of "flesh" and overlook the influence of the world and the devil, we will attempt to outwardly restrain our flesh. "Do not handle, do not taste, do not touch" (Colossians 2:21) will become the song that echoes through the hall of our existence. We will be consumed with law as a means to control our flesh and our lives will lack security and joy.

Although we have enemies, God has provided weapons for us. He has given us His Spirit, His Word and the Body (Chapter 7) to enable us to withstand the evil coalition that wages war against us. As believers we have victory over the world, the flesh and the devil through our faith in the substitutionary work of Jesus on Calvary. 1 John 4:4 says, "You are from God, little children, and have overcome them; because greater is He who is in you than he who is in the world."

THE ENEMIES AND THE NON-BELIEVER

Before leaving this chapter I feel compelled to include a section on the plight of the non-Christian. Non-believers live positionally on the left side of the Fork. They have a permanent residence in the domain of darkness. In many cases they are not even aware of the existence of the kingdom of light. They are oblivious to the reality of the right side of the Fork. Because they lack the Spirit of God, the gospel message remains hidden to them and they do not possess any abilities or resources to uncover its mystery (1 Corinthians 2:14 & Colossians 1:26,27). Their minds are hardened and trapped behind a veil which is only removed when a person turns to Christ (2 Corinthians 3:14,15). In the book of Isaiah, non-believers are described as prey, captives, prisoners, blind, lame, lost and brokenhearted.

As one imprisoned on the left side of the Fork, the non-Christian has only two options in behavior, ever. His life is an endless vacillation between the two faces of the flesh as he heeds the lies of the world, articulated to his heart by the devil. Existence is reduced to enslavement in licentiousness, legalism or continual fluctuation between the two.

I had a great uncle named Adrian, who was placed in an assisted living facility in our hometown in the early 1970's. Every Wednesday after school my Mother, brother and sisters and I would go over to visit him. We always brought him two things that were unavailable at the nursing home: chocolate and cigarettes. Uncle Adrian smoked a brand of cigarettes named "Lucky Strikes." During that era, it was still legal to advertise products containing tobacco. Perhaps you are old enough to remember an effective advertising campaign that Lucky Strikes conducted. In the television commercials, individuals sporting a black eye and clutching a cigarette between two fingers spouted the slogan, "I'd rather fight than switch!"

To fight or to switch, these are the only two options open to the non-Christian who abides on the left side of the Fork. First, he can fight. At some point in his existence, the non-believer will feel his need for significance. There is the desire to matter, to count and to be loved. Some have called this a "God shaped void in our hearts." Solomon, in Ecclesiastes 3:11, says that God has placed eternity in our hearts. By this he means that we have an innate longing for someone to love us with a perfect love. This desire is God given and is good in its intent to drive us to Him. But only God can fulfill that desire. At various moments in life, non-believers experience this pull on their hearts. This can occur when things begin to fall apart in life, when all immediate goals for life have been achieved and things are going well or when things in life settle to a place where busyness stops long enough for quiet introspection. Whatever the catalyst, when confronted with this yearning, one possible course of action is to "fight." This fight or increased intensity in effort can take place whether he is living licentiously or legalistically. He can either "buckle down" by recommitting to work harder at keeping the rules in an attempt to earn the significance he seeks, or he can delve deeper into his licentious lifestyle of law breaking to fulfill the elusive desire.

How does the legalist "fight?" Suppose there is a young man who is a junior in High School. He is diligent in turning in class assignments, studies effectively for tests and is earning good grades for his efforts. Yet he feels an emptiness within and convinces himself that he knows the answer. He will make all A's next semester. He is sure that this will remove the hollow feeling he is experiencing. So he attains this goal; still it is not enough. He decides he needs something more to recommend him as unique. So he pushes himself academically and achieves the highest numerical grade point average in his class. His discontent persists. He presses on and drives himself to acquire enough Advanced Placement credits to skip an entire semester of college. Still there must be more. He can never satisfy the god of academic achievement. What is going on with this young man? As viewed from the outside, his life is commendable. He has goals. He is diligent and studious. He is intelligent and is rewarded for his labors. But what is driving the behavior? His motivation is solely derived from a desire to earn or buy favor and worth. This is the plight of the legalist who endlessly pursues significance through traditionally acceptable standards.

How does the licentious person "fight?" Imagine a 16-year-old girl who feels insecure and desperately wants to "matter" to someone. She wants to feel special and know that there is someone who can provide the love that fairy tales promise. So, she dates. In order to keep her current boyfriend, when he presses her about having sex, she agrees. Still she is not experiencing the fulfillment of all her romantic expectations and the value they guaranteed her. She concludes that she must have selected the wrong guy. She establishes that she needs to date and sleep with a guy from the "in" crowd. So she dates and has sex with the captain of the football team. The feelings of incompleteness remain. She is puzzled and seeks advice from her girl friends. Now she has the answer! They have counseled her and the solution has become evident to her. She reminds herself of their advice, "Have sex with a college guy, then you'll be special and all of your dreams for love will come true!" And, of course, she will never find what she is looking for. Not because it is non-existent, but because she is looking in the wrong place. The fulfillment that she seeks is only in Christ. It is only available on the right side of the Fork. Yet the above scenario is the plight of the licentious person who incessantly seeks worth, value and love in law breaking.

Both of these scenarios are illustrated on the Fork in the following manner:

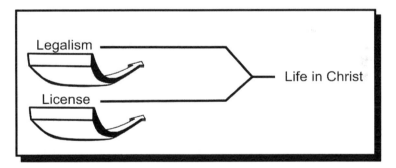

The "fight" strategy of the non-believer is to try harder at the tactic that they are already employing. The underlying assumption is that the strategy will work, but more energy, resources and effort need to be expended to achieve the desired results.

The second strategy employed by non-Christians is to "switch." When confronted with the lack of meaning in life or when experiencing the desire for worth, the non-believer may utilize the fight strategy. After giving everything that he has to achieve in this manner and still coming away empty handed, the logical conclusion is that it is the wrong strategy. Non-Christians see, for example, that academic excellence, even if achieved to the ultimate end, cannot fulfill. So the only alternative is to switch strategies. The problem is that there is only one other possibility; there is only one other "face" of the flesh to which they can turn.

How does a legalist "switch?" Let's suppose there is a respectable, church attending teenage female. Although a non-believer, she faithfully attends youth group activities. She feels an emptiness and is very dissatisfied with her life. She senses that there is something missing that there must be more to life than her present experience of it. So, she decides to try an alternate lifestyle; she resolves to "switch." So, she rebels against her parents' authority, reviews the church scene and realizes that she's "been there, done that," and begins to hang out with some kids from school that her parents disapprove of. These new friends have "loose morals" and have been rumored to be selling narcotics. She frantically throws herself into this new arena of law breaking, moving from a life of legalism to licentiousness. The void in her life that she was attempting to fill still looms larger and blacker than ever. The "switch" has not lived up to her expectations. Her life is meaningless and there seems to be no hope.

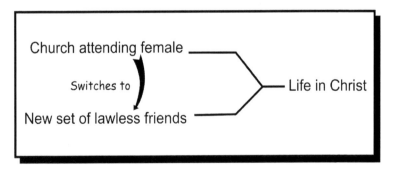

How does the licentious person "switch?" Let's imagine that there is a young man who is addicted to heroine. He is tired of the endless pursuit of the higher high, of having to lie and steal to obtain the money necessary to support his drug habit. He decides that there has to be more to life than this exhausting cycle of highs and lows, deceit and depression. So, he determines he will get his life "cleaned up" and admits himself to a drug rehab facility. After successfully completing the rehab program, he gets out and attempts to live drug free and in accordance with traditional values. He gets a job, which he hates, and tries to cultivate new relationships. Each day is an empty replica of the one that has gone before. There is no meaning or value in his being. The true purpose that he seeks eludes him and he lives in despair and hopelessness. Perhaps he returns to his drug use to escape from aimlessness of his existence.

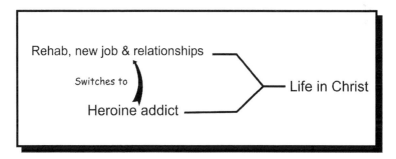

This is the dilemma of the non-believer. He lives in a vicious cycle of vacillation between the two faces of the flesh and has no hope of finding the love and worth he seeks on the left side of the fork. It is not there.

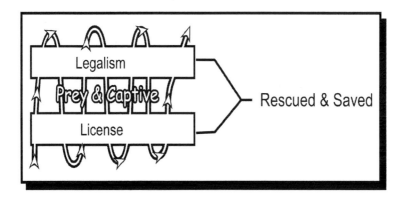

In Ephesians 2:12 Paul reminds Christians that we too, were once living this existence. He says, "Remember that you were at that time separate from Christ, excluded from the commonwealth of Israel, and strangers to the covenants of promise, *having no hope and without God in the world"* (emphasis mine). The Old Testament speaks of the unsaved as prisoners of war. Isaiah 49:24-25 says, "Can the prey be taken from the mighty man or the captives of the tyrant be rescued?" Hope for the lost is found in the message of Isaiah as he continues, "Surely thus says the Lord, 'Even the captives of the mighty man will be taken away and the prey of the tyrant will be rescued. For I will contend with the one who contends with you and I will save your sons.'" Freedom from the domain of darkness was obtained at the Cross. God is a God of redemption, and He is the only One who is able to contend with the enemy and secure victory and hope for man.

Let us not forget that as those who rest in Christ for our salvation we have an "out" from the plight faced by the non-believer described above. There is a third way for us. The gospel message ensures us a place of freedom and a life of largeness. We are loved with a perfect love. We matter to the only One whose opinion really counts. We are so valuable to Him that He was willing to sacrifice that which was most precious to His heart, His Son, for us. In the Father's eyes we are beautiful, holy and blameless and beyond reproach. When we know these truths, really know them in a practical way, they free us from the endless volleying between license and legalism. No longer are we like a tennis ball, batted here and there by the trials and circumstances of life. We are free to dwell secure in our Father's love and bask in His delight over us. Our enemies are defeated and the victory is ours.

We have looked at two of our resources, the Spirit and the Word of God, on the Fork. We have surveyed our enemies, the World, the Flesh and the Devil and visually depicted them there as well. But there is one additional resource given to believers by the Father that needs further exploration. Let's move on and examine the Body of Christ and where it fits on the Fork Illustration.

Chapter 7
The Body on the Fork Illustration

In direct opposition to the three-member coalition of enemies that believers have are the three interdependent spiritual assets of the Word, the Spirit and the Body. God has specifically equipped His people with resources to withstand the offensive attacks of the world, the flesh and the devil.

Thus far we have looked at the two faces of the flesh on the Fork Illustration. We have also seen the two mutually exclusive sources to which humans look for truth. The lies of the world are pitted against the truth of the Word of God as a competing yet mutually exclusive lens through which we interpret life and reality. In addition, we have examined the two conflicting "voices" which seek to influence the human heart. One voice is that of a liar and slanderer, the devil. The contrasting message flows from the Spirit of truth. What does this model lack for completion? What is the missing piece?

When we were saved we were united to Christ. While it is true that we were united to him as individuals, we were also simultaneously united to a community of believers. This community, the church, is a new humanity in Christ. 1 Peter 2:9-10 says, "But you are a chosen race, a royal priesthood, a holy nation, a people for God's own possession, that you may proclaim the excellencies of Him who has called you out of darkness into His marvelous light; for once you were not the people of God; you had not received mercy, but now you have received mercy." Peter clearly links our having received mercy from God with our becoming part of the people of God.

We have been looking at the Fork Illustration through a culturally limited grid of "self." Western culture is individualized in its perspective. We are so used to viewing circumstances and relationships through a personalized grid that we are like fish in water. Fish are unaware of water. Because it surrounds them and has always been a part of their experience, they are oblivious to its presence. Like the fish that does not even recognize the existence of the water, we are usually unaware that we carry our egocentric perception of reality into our relationship with the church. Edmund Clowney expresses it this way: "American evangelicals have a tradition of individualism that sees the church as a voluntary club for the converted. We don't have a deep Biblical sense of our corporate identity."[1] The emphasis thus far has been on how Christianity affects us individually. What has happened to *me*? How do *I* receive power for change in *my* life? But as Peter explains in this passage, our individual union with Christ has much broader and comprehensive implications.

While we see God interacting with and through individuals throughout Scripture, it is always within the context of His redemptive purposes for mankind. God has an overarching plan and is working all things "after the counsel of His will" (Ephesians 1:11). Within this eternal design, He has chosen to deal with man through covenantal mediation. He has also chosen to call out a people for His own possession. As Dr. Douglas Kelly reminds us, "The central theme in covenant blessing throughout all history is (Revelation 21:3), 'I will be your God and you will be my *people*"[2] (emphasis mine). While we are singularly united to Christ by faith in a covenantal union, no individual person can be "a *people*."

Webster's Dictionary defines community as "a group of people living together as a smaller social unit...and having interests, work, etc. in common."[3] Believers operate interdependently as we endeavor to live holy lives and grow in the grace and knowledge of the Lord and His gospel message. The Body is recognized as one of our resources because life on the right side of the Fork is a life of faith. This existence implies increased awareness in one's state of absolute bankruptcy apart from Jesus. To be human is to be spiritually blind. We all need help from outside of ourselves to see our sin, cast ourselves upon Christ and seek the intervention of the Spirit to withstand the spiritual enemies of the world, the flesh and the devil. Our gracious Father has seen fit to provide us with brothers and sisters, equipped with the Spirit and Word of

God, who come along side of us, remove our spiritual blindfolds and bring the truth to light. Our new family encourages us in our faith.

When we stumble and fall into functional "left side living," the Spirit of God can directly work within our hearts to both call to mind and to apply the Word hidden within, to produce repentance and faith. In addition, He can use non-believers, or even nature itself, to remind us of the gospel message and of our identity in the Savior. But more often than not, He uses a Christian brother or sister to speak the message of grace into our lives. Why? Because the church is the community of grace. By and large, the world knows little, if nothing about grace. In the parable of the Prodigal Son, Luke tells us that while the younger son was in the field feeding a Gentile's swine that he was "...longing to fill his stomach with the pods that the swine were eating, and *no one was giving anything to him*" (verse 16, emphasis mine). The world does not give anything for free. Americans even have a saying, "You get what you pay for." When confronted with an expression of grace, most are too busy skeptically looking for the "attached string" to be gripped by the concept of grace underlying the offering. Those who are part of the true church of Jesus Christ understand what grace is about. They are first hand witnesses of the existence and power of grace and as such are uniquely qualified to remind fellow family members of its wonder. Even though we are given no specifics on how the Prodigal Son was awakened to the reality of his situation, we can be sure that by the faithful intervention of other members of the Body *we* are often "brought to our senses" and return from the far country. We are part of a group of people who have common interests, principally including the fact that we are fellow participants in the grace of God.

In Philippians 1, Paul says that he is committed to praying for the saints at Philippi. He expresses concern over their spiritual well being and says that "...it is only right for me to feel this way about you all, because I have you in my heart...you all are partakers of grace with me"

(Philippians 1:7). As believers we share in God's amazing grace.

In Ephesians 2:11-22 the apostle Paul provides foundational teaching on the church,

> Therefore remember, that formerly you, the Gentiles in the flesh, who are called "Uncircumcision" by the so-called 'Circumcision,' which is performed in the flesh by human hands--remember that you were at that time separate from Christ, excluded from the commonwealth of Israel, and strangers to the covenants of promise, having no hope and without God in the world. But now in Christ Jesus you who formerly were far off have been brought near by the blood of Christ. For He Himself is our peace, who made both groups into one, and broke down the barrier of the dividing wall, by abolishing in His flesh the enmity, which is the Law of commandments contained in ordinances, that in Himself He might make the two into one new man, thus establishing peace, and might reconcile them both in one body to God through the Cross, by it having put to death the enmity. And He came and preached peace to you who were far away, and peace to those who were near; for through Him we both have our access in one Spirit to the Father. So then, you are no longer strangers and aliens, but you are fellow citizens with the saints, and are of God's household, having been built on the foundation of the apostles and prophets, Christ Jesus Himself being the corner stone, in whom the whole building, being fitted together is growing into a holy temple in the Lord; in whom you also are being built together into a dwelling of God in the Spirit.

This passage tells us that if we have been brought near through the blood of Christ, then we have been grafted into one new man. We have become fellow citizens with the saints and are now members of God's household. Not only did He save us individually, but we have also been adopted into a family.

Suppose that a woman marries a man who was raised in foster homes. He was orphaned at birth and has no family at all. When she unites herself to him, the union is limited to her and the man. This is a picture of how many American Christians subconsciously view their salvation. As individualistic moderns, we selectively see only the fact that we have been united to Christ. While our union with Him is wondrous and provides the basis for our acceptance before the Father, freedom from the penalty of sin and promise of a personal on-going work of sanctification within us because of the resulting indwelling Holy Spirit, to restrict that union to a "me and Him" entity is to lose incredible blessing and tremendous power and resources that come as we are connected to the Body of Christ.

A better illustration of the reality of our union with Christ would be a woman who marries a widower who has four children. All of his children still live at home. His widowed mother lives in his basement apartment. His single brother lives in the attic flat. When she marries the widower, does she marry the man? Yes, but she also marries his family. Her marriage contract binds her to him, but it also connects her to both the benefits and responsibilities of his extended family.

This same idea is also depicted for us by Jesus in Matthew 5:14. Americans are programmed to view life through a personal perspective. I recently saw a commercial for a national car rental company. The advertisement was expounding the virtues of the company's "on-line, by-pass the counter, no waiting in line, choose your own make and color vehicle, all about 'me' click-click click services" currently available to the public. The life of the average U.S. citizen is far too often "all about me." The "default" of our flesh to "look out for number one." We carry this paradigm over not only into how we regard Christianity as a whole, but also into how we read Scripture. For example, when we read, "You are the light of the world..." we culturally interpret this to mean that we are personally to bear testimony of God's work of grace in our lives to those around us. We are prone to imagine ourselves to be individual candles that illuminate the darkness of our world. We disconnect this first part of the Matthew 5:14 from the second half of the verse which says, "A city set on a hill cannot be hidden." When we are able to step out of our culturally narrow frame of reference, we are enabled to comprehend the actual intent of the verse. "You (plural, i.e., you, the Body of Christ) are the light of the world. A city set on a hill cannot be hidden." Just as we saw in the I Peter passage that a person cannot be a "people," neither can an individual be a *city.*

A person can easily go undetected, but a city cannot be overlooked. While a single candle can be ignored, a raging bonfire does not go unnoticed. It is true that in the moment of our justification we are "lit" with the fire of Christ, but we are not merely a single flame. In our unity with His body, we are part of a spectacular pyrotechnic display that the world cannot disregard. Non-believers who witness behaviors by individual believers that are driven by kingdom values may dismiss the actions as mere eccentricity. But when the church functions in unity as designed by Christ, the resulting character and service are inexplicable. Ed Clowney explains it this way: "Individual testimony to Christ's lordship and kingdom wins only a shrug...the church, however, as the community of Christ's kingdom can show the world an ethical integrity it must respect."[4]

As believers we are part of a "chosen race." A race is a group of people connected by blood.[5] Christians are indeed connected by blood, not the blood that courses through our veins, but the blood of Christ that covers our sins. We often hear the proverb that "blood is thicker than water." Research into the origin of this proverb turned up the following quote: "This phrase has completely lost is original, covenant-related, meaning. Today it is interpreted as meaning that blood-related family members are to be considered as more important than anyone else. However, the original meaning is, 'The blood of the covenant is thicker than the water of the womb,' or, 'My relationship with those to whom I am joined in covenant is to be considered of more value than the relationship with a brother with whom I may have shared the womb.'"[6] It is highly possible that this phrase, while not specifically found in Scripture, has it roots in the concept of blood covenants found therein. Regardless of its origin, the emphasis is on the fact that a bond of blood is stronger than any other, and believers share a blood bond in Christ.

When we were non-believers we lived in the flesh. All of life was focused on self. Every thought, word, deed and motivation was directed toward the advancement, enhancement, maintenance and enlargement of self.[7] "We" were all that we had, and we were consequently self-absorbed. We were consumed with our own needs, trials and interests. Occupying the position of universal centrality was our primary goal. Our *legalistic* tendency was to position ourselves as our own Savior through law keeping. Our *licentious* tendency was to position ourselves as our own Master or Lord through law breaking. In either case, all behaviors were in reference to "me" and were driven by fear and pride. All actions were attempts to overcome guilt and shame through *self-effort* or *self-rule*.

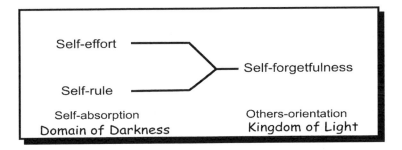

But when we were transferred to the kingdom of light, God dealt with our shame and guilt. He provided the satisfaction for the deepest longing of our hearts. He loves us perfectly. We need not fear, ever (1 John 4:18). In Christ He sees us as beautiful and pure, in spite of our guilt and shame. We no longer need to seek beauty and righteousness of our own. (Isaiah 1:18 "'Come now, and let us reason together,' says the Lord, 'Though your sins are as scarlet, they will be as white as snow; though they are red like crimson, they will be like wool.'") In the acknowledgement of our sin and neediness, our pride is broken and therefore ceases to be a driving factor. The reasons that previously motivated all self-centered behavior and self-absorption have been invalidated. They are no longer relevant. There no longer remains any excuse for us to live self-centered lives. We are now full and free to focus outwardly and be "others-centered" rather than "self-centered." Behavior can now be driven by faith, humility and love. We are liberated to live for "community" and to fulfill God's purposes for the church.

Scripture uses many metaphors to describe the church. In the Old Testament, "Israel is God's son, His spouse, His vine, His flock. In the New Testament, the church is Christ's flock, branches of the true vine, his bride, his body, his temple, the dwelling of the Holy Spirit, the house of God."[8] Because the image of the Body of Christ is so prominent and most easily illustrated, it is used as the graphic representation of the church in the Fork Illustration. It can be drawn on the Fork as follows:

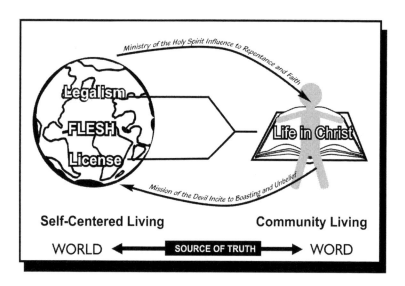

After knowing only self-obsessed living in the flesh, we are now called to community in the Spirit of Christ. The church is a radically different, others-centered society.

THE CHURCH: DEFINITION

The church is the community of the Word. It is gathered by the Word and has been commanded by her head, Christ, to exercise various sacraments that are marks or evidences to the world of its existence. While our flesh had two recognizable faces dedicated to serving "self," the church has three identifiable faces devoted to serving God and others. These faces can be designated as her Upward, Inward and Outward profiles. The Upward face of the church is her service of worship. The Inward face is her service of nurture of believers. And her Outward face is her service of outreach or mission to the non-believing world. All three of these faces are essential to a vital church. If any one of the three is absent or even anemic, all three are, to some extent, diminished. These three faces are illustrated as follows:

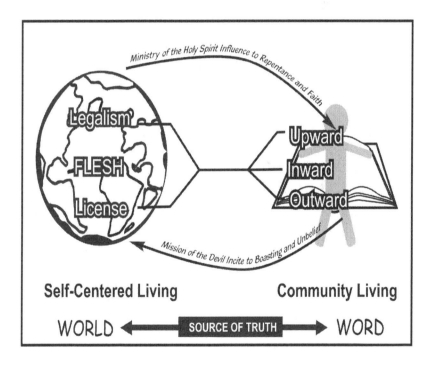

The Upward face of worship is the service of the church by which she gives God centrality in all. By design, humans are created for worship. We all worship something, every minute of every day. God calls the church to worship Him. He does not do so out of some distorted sense of megalomania, but rather for our benefit. When we worship anything other than God Himself, we become idolaters. Without Christ centered worship, the church is indistinguishable from any other social assembling of individuals. She could just as well be the routine gathering of country club members for a community service project.

The Inward face of nurture is the aspect of body life in which the church seeks maturity of her members, the measure of the stature which belongs to the fullness of Christ (Ephesians 4:13). This growth is a process and is done interdependently. We only grow individually as we grow corporately. Colossians 2:19 says, "...holding fast to the head, from whom the entire body, being supplied and held together by the joints and ligaments, grows with a growth which is from God." Of this verse Hendricksen notes that "the main idea is that to Christ the entire church owes its growth...Just as the human body, when properly supported and held together by joints and ligaments, experiences normal growth, so also the church, when each of its members supports and maintains loving contact with the others, will, under the sustaining care of God, proceed from grace to grace and glory to glory."[9] Without the service of nurture of the believers, the church would be a gathering of infants. Infants are incredibly needy and are unable to function reproductively. As such, without nurture there could be no outreach.

The Outward face of mission is the ministry of the Body to those apart from Christ. It is the incarnation of His Word to a hurting and dying world. Christ's last instructions to His disciples included His Great Commission to go and make disciples of all the nations, to go into all the world and preach the gospel to all creation. Without an Outward face portraying acts of mercy and speaking words of grace, the local church becomes self-focused and ingrown. As such, she is characterized by factions and divisions, which if left unresolved, frequently lead to her demise.

Just as the *world* was central in influencing the self-centered individual, now the *Word* of God is central in all areas of service for the Body. The Word is at the heart of our worship. In addition, the Word is the bread of life that we break with one another for nourishment and growth. It is also the seed that we sow in the world which produces a harvest among the nations. In *The Church*, Ed Clowney says,

> In every task of the church, the ministry of the Word of God is central. It is the Word that calls us to worship, addresses us in worship, teaches us how to worship and enables us to praise God and to encourage one another. By the Word we are given life and nurtured to maturity in Christ: the Word is the sword of the Spirit to correct us and the bread of the Spirit to feed us. In the mission of the church, it is the Word of God that calls the nations to the Lord: in the teaching of the Word we make disciples of the nations. The growth of the church is the growth of the Word....[10]

Dr. Clowney goes on to say that the church is the "...community of believers showing the root of faith in the fruit of love."[11] As such, life within the church (life on the right side of the Fork) differs from existence under the domain of darkness (life on the left side of the Fork) because it is organized for service, not selfishness; building up others, not shoring up self; giving to my neighbor, not getting for myself; encouraging one another, not enhancing "me"; edifying others, not enlarging my interests; and external ministry, not internal maintenance and promotion. The world does not understand the upside down, inside out value system of God's economy. To its way of thinking, people who hold to these ideals are "losers." Indeed, "The church is composed of losers – those who have lost everything for Christ's sake, but have found everything in Him."[12]

The church is enabled to carry out the Upward, Inward and Outward triad of ministries because of the indwelling Holy Spirit. In and of herself the Body of Christ has no power and is inadequate for the task assigned by her Head. But God has provided the necessary catalyst to accomplish her mission. "The greatest resource in building Christ's church is the gift of the Holy Spirit."[13] Undeniably, life on the right side of the Fork *is* life in the Spirit. Because He is the Spirit of Christ, indwelt believers are equipped with Christ's ministry abilities (Spiritual gifts) and evidence Christ's character (Spiritual fruit).

1 Corinthians 12:7 tells us, "But to each one is given the manifestation of the Spirit for the common good." Spiritual gifts are given to believers to be employed in the edification of the entire body. All gifts are valuable and necessary. It is only as individual members exercise gifts for corporate health and growth that the kingdom of God is advanced here on earth. We grow together or not at all: "...the church *together* seeks maturity, 'attaining to the whole measure of the fullness of Christ.' *Together* we grow up into him who is the Head, that is, Christ" (Ephesians 4:13,15, emphasis mine).

Believers are familiar with the gifts of the Spirit and know well the passages that describe them to us (Romans 12, Ephesians 4, 1 Corinthians 12 and 1 Peter 4). As is our habit, we read these passages through a self-filter. We become absorbed with the question, "Which manifestation of the Spirit is mine?" In our quest for gift disclosure we not only lose sight of the corporate emphasis, but also of the very nature of the gift. We forget that the Spirit *Himself* is the gift. Acts 8:19-20 says, "Now when Simon saw that the Spirit was bestowed through the laying on of the apostles' hands, he offered them money, saying, 'Give this authority to me as well, so that everyone on whom I lay my hands may receive the **Holy Spirit**.' But Peter said to him, 'May your silver perish with you, because you thought you could obtain the **gift** of God with money'" (emphasis mine). The exercise of spiritual gifts benefits the body. Just as our physical bodies are weakened by lack of exercise, when members of the Body refrain from exercising their spiritual gifts, the effectiveness of the Body is diminished.

In addition to receiving ministry abilities through spiritual gifts, members of His Body manifest the character of Christ through spiritual fruit. Galatians 5:22-23 lists some of the fruit of the Spirit: "But the fruit of the Spirit is love, joy, peace, patience, kindness, goodness, faithfulness, gentleness, self-control; against such things there is no law." Other spiritual fruit are compassion, humility, hope or generosity. Life in the Spirit includes expression of the person of Christ, which is the fruit of the Spirit. The fruit of the Spirit is love, and it is love that binds us together as a family. One expression of this love is peace. Because we have peace with God, we have peace with fellow members of His body. Fruit unites us with other believers.

While both the fruit and the gifts originate with the Spirit and are both visible and necessary within the Body, they are functionally different. "The graces of the Spirit (fruit), on the one hand, make us like Christ and like one another as we grow in faith, hope and love. The gifts of the Spirit, on the other hand, distinguish us from one another, qualifying us for distinct ministries in the service of Christ."[14] Fruit is what we hold in common. Our character is similar because it is a reflection of the *nature* of our Savior. Gifts are what make us diverse. Our functions are varied because they are a reflection of the manifold *abilities* of our Savior.

The fruit and the gifts of the Spirit are evidenced in each aspect of service within the Body. For both gifts and fruit to glorify Christ they must function simultaneously. The Apostle Paul speaks eloquently to this in 1 Corinthians 13:1-3:

> If I speak with the tongues of men and of angels, but do not have love, I have become a noisy gong or a clanging cymbal. And if I have the gift of prophecy, and know all mysteries and all knowledge; and if I have all faith, so as to remove mountains, but do not have love, I am nothing. And if I give all of my possessions to feed the poor, and if I deliver my body to be burned, but do not have love, it profits me nothing.

Here Paul explains that exercising spiritual gifts such as tongues, prophecy, knowledge, faith or giving without the accompanying fruit of love is of no value. While gifts and fruit are distinctly different, they are interdependent in their expression. "When the gifts are in any way detached from the fruit of the Spirit in the service of love they become distracting noise, attracting attention but accomplishing nothing."[15] As such they are placed on the Fork as follows:

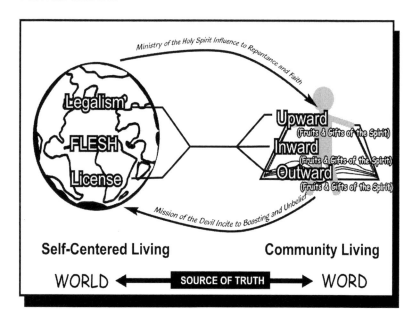

In addition to supplying the Body with the gifts and fruit of the Spirit, God provided three marks that enable the Body to be readily identified and recognized in the world. These distinguishing marks include the proclamation of the Word of God, administration of the sacraments, and the appropriate exercise of church discipline.

An obvious sign of a local manifestation of the Body of Christ is the proclamation of the Word of God. The local church has a message that is central to its existence. The Scripture is read and taught as the church gathers corporately. The declaration of the good news of salvation for sinners through the death of a substitute is a sign that identifies the church in the world. "The great mark of the church is in the message it proclaims: the gospel of salvation from sin and eternal death through the Cross and resurrection of Jesus Christ, who alone is the Way, the Truth and the Life."[16]

The sacraments are the means by which people practically get in touch with God.[17] The title of this book is

The Gospel for the Visual Learner. While the Fork is merely a man-made graphic to depict the truths of the gospel, God has given the Body the gospel in visual form in the sacraments to remind believers of what He has done for us in Christ. Although we are united with Christ, our union is not something we can see or touch. Because of the abstractness of this union, God has given us sacraments so that we can better identify and connect with Him. Dr. Kelly expresses it this way: "Because our union with Christ is mysterious and intangible, God appointed two tangible signs which we can comprehend with our five senses, for us to have a more concrete representation of that union."[18] In both the Lord's Supper and in Baptism we have a visual reminder of our union with Christ through His sacrificial atonement. In addition to these sacraments being visual, we taste the bread and wine of the Lord's Supper. We feel them with our hands as we grasp the cup and wafer or bread portion. We smell the grapes and the wheat. In Baptism we feel or hear the water being administered. Although we experience God through faith, in His wisdom God provided means for us to have sensory friendly reminders of His work on our behalf.

The sacraments are a second mark that identifies the church in the world. Edmund Clowney explains the identification as follows: "In Baptism we are numbered among the children, receiving the name of our Father, written as it were, on our foreheads."[19] When we undergo or witness Baptism we are reminded that we belong to a family. Both those within and without the church recognize baptism as a mark of membership. Those who are baptized are identified with the community of Christ

Because we live in a wealthy society, most of us are blessed enough to be able to enjoy supper daily. Even the simplest of us realizes that we need to be fed to sustain our life, so God gives us the Lord's Supper – the visual representation that only His nourishment sustains us spiritually. Only our union with Christ, the Bread of Life, imparts and sustains our life. In Jewish society wine was a symbol of joy. When we partake of the cup as we participate in the Lord's Supper we are reminded of the joy of our salvation that is made possible by the shed blood of Jesus on our behalf. The celebration of the Lord's Supper both looks back to the Cross, reminding us of our justification, and looks forward to the Wedding Feast of the Lamb, bringing to mind our future glorification.

The church of the New Testament is not alone in its need for visual reminders of God's work on her behalf. In the Old Testament, Israel repeatedly forgot God. In order to help the Jews remember His power and grace to them, God commanded that Israel celebrate festivals such as the Feast of Booths and the Passover.

We are a stubborn, absent-minded people. We are prone to self-concentration and forgetfulness. As such, we need daily encouragement lest we become "hardened by the deceitfulness of sin" (Hebrews 3:13). As His children, God graciously gives us each other to remind us of the hope of His calling and the riches of the glory of His inheritance in the saints.

Chapter 8
Speaking to Yourself with "Fork" Tongue

Regardless of whether we are cognizant of the fact or not, we live every minute of every day of our lives in one of the three positions depicted on the Fork Illustration. In union with Christ, the believer "lives" by the Spirit, but does not always walk that way. In Galatians 5:25 Paul reminds us, "If we live by the Spirit, let us also walk by the Spirit." Life on the right side of the Fork is a life of faith. Faith not only gives us spiritual life, but Romans 1:17 says that the righteous man shall *live* by faith. Indeed, the writer of Hebrews tells us that without faith, it is impossible to please God. In this we see that life on the left side of the Fork *cannot* please God. If our goal is to remain or abide on the right side, or at least to grow in the amount of time we spend actually living there, we need to know how that is accomplished.

To live out of who we are in Christ, we must be mindful of our identity in Him. Abiding or remaining in Him is how we accomplish right side living. This is achieved by reminding ourselves of the gospel. In the preface to his book, *The Discipline of Grace*, Jerry Bridges makes the following comment: "I also owe a debt of gratitude to my friend, Dr. Jack Miller, from whom I acquired the expression, 'Preaching the gospel to yourself everyday.'"[1] Both Jerry Bridges and Jack Miller are calling this reminder of our covenantal relationship with God "preaching the gospel to yourself." Another way of saying this that would relate to the illustration presented in this book is to "speak to yourself with Forked Tongue." It is the idea that we are to remember who we truly are in Christ. Our true identity is tied up with our relationship in Him.

To whom are we to "speak with Forked Tongue?" In Psalm 42:5-6 we find the psalmist speaking to himself. He addresses his own heart as follows: "Why are you in despair, O my soul and why have you become disturbed within me? Hope in God, for I shall again praise Him for the help of His presence. O my God, my soul is in despair within me; therefore I *remember* Thee from the land of the Jordan, and the peaks of Hermon, from Mount Mizar." Not only do we need to remind ourselves of the gospel daily, but we are also called to "encourage one another day after day...lest any one of you be hardened by the deceitfulness of sin" (Hebrews 3:13).

We need constant reminders because we are a forgetful people. In the Old Testament the word *shakah*, meaning "to forget," is used 102 times. The authors of the *Theological Word Book of the Old Testament* make the following comment on the usage of *shakah*:

> It is in God and man's reciprocal relationship that the verb *shakah* finds its most steady use.... More often man is the subject of *shakah*, the one who forgets. Forgetting is not simply a psychological act of having a thought pass from one's consciousness, a temporary or permanent lapse in memory. This is indicated by the frequent identification of the verb with an action.[2]

When tracing this word through the Old Testament, the most overwhelmingly prominent action associated with forgetting God is idolatry. As discussed in Chapter 5, idolatry is the worship of anything other than God and is the root of all behavior flowing out of life on the left side of the Fork. The following references are just a sample, yet provide ample evidence to support the claim that there is an undeniable link between idolatry and "forgetting God."

- Deuteronomy 4:23 "So watch yourselves, lest you **forget** the covenant of the Lord your God, which He made with you, and make for yourselves a *graven image* in the form of anything against which the Lord your God has commanded you."

- Deuteronomy 8:18-19 "But you shall **remember** the Lord your God, for it is He who is giving you power to make wealth, that He may confirm His covenant which He swore to your fathers, as it is this day. And it shall come about if you ever **forget** the Lord your God, and go after *other gods* and serve them and worship them, I shall testify against you today that you shall surely perish."

- Deuteronomy 32:16-18 "They made Him jealous with *strange gods*; with abominations they provoked Him to anger. They sacrificed to demons who were not God, to *gods* whom they have not know, *new gods* who came lately, whom your fathers did not dread. You neglected the Rock who begot you, and **forgot** the God who gave you birth."

- Judges 3:7 "And the sons of Israel did what was evil in the sight of the Lord, and **forgot** the Lord their God and *served the Baals and the Asheroth*."

- Judges 8:33-34 "Then it came about, as soon as Gideon was dead, that the sons of Israel, again played the harlot with the *Baals,* and made *Baal-berith their god*. Thus the sons of Israel **did not remember** the Lord their God, who had delivered them from the hands of all their enemies on every side...."

- 1 Samuel 12:9-10 "But they **forgot** the Lord their God, so He sold them into the hand of Sisera, captain of the army of Hazor, and into the hand of the Philistines and into the hand of the King of Moab, and they fought against them. And they cried out to the Lord and said, 'We have sinned because we have forsaken the Lord and have *served the Baals and the Asheroth*; but now deliver us from the hands of our enemies, and we will serve Thee.'"

- Isaiah 57:11 & 13 "Of whom were you worried and fearful, when you lied and **did not remember** Me, nor give Me a thought? ... When you cry out, let your collection of *idols* deliver you. But the wind will carry all of them up, and a breath will take them away. But he who takes refuge in Me shall inherit the land, and shall possess My holy mountain."

- Jeremiah 23:27 (God is speaking of the false prophets in Israel) "...who intend to make My people **forget** My name by their dreams which they dream which they relate to one another, just as their fathers **forgot** My name because of *Baal*."

- Hosea 2:13 "'And I will punish her for the days of the *Baals* when she used to offer sacrifices to them and adorn herself with her earrings and jewelry, and follow her lovers, so that she **forgot** Me,' declares the Lord."

- Isaiah 17:10 "For you have **forgotten** the God of your salvation and have not remembered the rock of your refuge. Therefore you plant delightful plants and set them with vine slips of a *strange god.*"

- Jeremiah 2:26-28 & 32 "As the thief is shamed when he is discovered, so the house of Israel is shamed; they, their kings, their princes and their priests, and their prophets, who say to a tree, 'You are my father,' and to a stone, 'You gave me birth.' For they have turned their back to Me and not their face; but in the time of trouble they will say, 'Arise and save us.' But where are your *gods* which you have made for yourself? Let them arise, if they can save you in the time of your trouble; for according to the number of your cities are your gods, O Judah.... Can a virgin forget her ornaments, or a bride her attire? Yet My people have **forgotten** Me days without number."

- Jeremiah 18:15 "For My people have **forgotten** Me, they burn incense to *worthless gods* and they have stumbled from their ways, from the ancient paths, to walk in bypaths, not on the highway...."

The book of Deuteronomy is all about "reminding." After 40 years of wilderness wandering, God told Moses to write it for the new generation of Israelites who were about to enter the promised land. He knew that man's heart is "prone to wander and leave the God he loves." God wanted to ensure that Israel was reminded of who He is, what He had done for them, what He had promised them in the covenant He'd made with their forefathers, and what He required of them. In Deuteronomy 31:14-22, Moses converses with God. God informs Moses that the time of Moses' death is near and instructs him to bring Joshua to the tent of meeting for commissioning. When Moses and Joshua arrive, God appears to them and foretells Israel's future idolatry. He says, "...this people will arise and play the harlot with the strange gods of the land, into the midst of which they are going, and will forsake Me and break My covenant which I have made with them." Of this verse Peter C. Craigie says, "The words of God are not primarily prophetic; they portray rather divine insight into the basic character of the people and their constant tendency to unfaithfulness."[3] How heavy Moses' heart must have been after hearing not only that he was to die without entering the promised land, but also learning that Israel would fall away and follow after false gods. In verse 19 God says, "Now therefore, write this song for yourselves, and teach it to the sons of Israel; put it on their lips, in order that this song may be a witness for Me against the sons of Israel." Verse 22 says, "So Moses wrote this song the same day and taught it to the sons of Israel." The song of Moses is then recorded in Deuteronomy 32:1-43. Craigie goes on to say:

> The song was to be remembered from one generation to the next and was never to be forgotten. It would serve as a warning of the dangers that would constantly beset Israel, perhaps preventing the people from going astray.... God perceived the intentions latent in the hearts of his people, even before they were themselves fully aware of them. But the goodness of God is perceived in the gift of the song, for a part of its function would be to warn the people of their emerging intentions and turn them back to God before it was too late. The role of the Song of Moses in the life of ancient Israel portrays clearly at least one of the roles the Bible plays in our Christian life in the modern world.[4]

God knew that Israel would forget Him and He made provision for their spiritual dementia. Because we possess the same disposition as our spiritual ancestors, God has similarly made provision for us. He has given us His Spirit, His Word and His people to "sing" the message of grace into our absentminded souls.

Scripture provides us with an example of how King David, the author of numerous Psalms, reminded himself of the gospel. It is a wonderful picture of how he spoke to himself with "Forked Tongue."

Psalm 103 is a general psalm of David. Although many of his psalms were written in the midst of either trial or jubilation in his life, there is no indication that there was a specific occasion for his writing Psalm 103. And while Deuteronomy 32 was a reminder by Moses to all of God's people of His gracious intervention in their lives, Psalm 103 is a reminder by King David to his own soul of what God has done for him. Psalm 103 says,

> Bless the Lord, O my soul; and all that is within me, bless His holy name. Bless the Lord, O my soul, and forget none of His benefits; who pardons all your iniquities; who heals all your diseases; who redeems your life from the pit; who crowns you with lovingkindness and compassion; who satisfies your years with good things, so that your youth is renewed like the eagle. The Lord performs righteous deeds, and judgments for all who are oppressed. He made known His ways to Moses, His acts to the sons of Israel. The Lord is compassionate and gracious, slow to anger and abounding in lovingkindness. He will not always strive with us; nor will He keep His anger forever. He has not dealt with us according to our iniquities. For as high as the heavens are above the earth, so great is His lovingkindness toward those who fear Him. As far as the east is from the west, so far has He removed our transgression from us. Just as a father has compassion on his children, so the Lord has compassion on those who fear Him. For He Himself knows our frame; He is mindful that we are but dust. As for man, his days are like grass; as a flower of the field, so he flourishes. When the wind passes over it, it is no more; and its place acknowledges it no longer. But the lovingkindness of the Lord is from everlasting to everlasting on those who fear Him and His righteousness to children's children, to those who keep His covenant, and who remember His precepts to do them. The Lord has established His throne in the heavens; and His sovereignty rules over all. Bless the Lord, you His angels, mighty in strength, who perform His word, obeying the voice of His word! Bless the Lord, all you His hosts, you who serve Him, doing His will. Bless the Lord, all you works of His, in all places of His dominion; bless the Lord, O my soul!

In Psalm 103 David is reminding himself of all that God has done for him. He is, in essence, preaching the gospel to himself or speaking with forked tongue. David is overwhelmed with the magnitude of God's goodness as evidenced by the use of the word "all" six times within 22 verses. In this psalm David catalogs all of the blessings or benefits of God's grace to him. He begins in verse 3 by saying that God has pardoned all of his iniquities and healed his diseases. David is right to begin with forgiveness. It is foundational and should be first because without peace with God he would possess none of His other benefits. Though it is found later in the psalm, David expands his memory of God's forgiveness by providing a word picture to express the magnitude of the pardon he has received. In verse 12 he says that God has removed our sin from us as far as the east is from the west. Of course we all realize that east and west are opposite directions. They are locationally mutually exclusive positions and illustrate how completely our sin has been removed from us. Additional commentary on this image is presented by James Montgomery Boice. Concerning verse 12, he says, "The psalmist is trying to point out that 'however many miles you think lie between west and east, you cannot look two ways at once.' You have to turn your back on one in order to look in the directions of the other. When God forgives us, he puts our sin and us on two different horizons. So when he looks at our sin, he is no longer looking at us, and when he looks at us, he is no longer looking at our sin. To use the vocabulary of Paul, he has justified us."[5] David begins by reminding himself that he has forgiveness and peace with God.

In verse 4 David moves on and reminds his soul that it has been redeemed from the pit. In the Old Testament the "pit" is Sheol. It was the place where the people were believed to go after dying. Here David is reminding himself of what he has been delivered *from*. He is mindful that this could have been his fate and, in fact, was the destiny he deserved, yet instead he says that God has crowned him with lovingkindness and compassion.

The lovingkindness of God is another repeated theme in this Psalm. David pens this word four times to remind himself that God's love is the ultimate cause of His grace and the basis for all of His bountiful acts on David's behalf. While it is true that we are saved by grace through faith, the underlying reason for the extension of God's grace is His love. David doesn't want to forget that the nature of God is love.

David concludes the first portion of this psalm with the reminder that not only has God forgiven and rescued him, but He has opened His hand to "satisfy his years with good things." As part of God's family, David experiences the goodness of God's abundant provision for him. Sometime those "good" things may not have looked very positive, but, by faith, David knew that God was good to him, all of the time.

In verses 6-18, although David is still speaking to his own soul, he is now reminding himself of what God has done for Israel. Not only do we need to remember what God has done for us as individuals, but we are also encouraged and motivated to right side living as we recall what He has done for His people collectively. We looked at this in Chapter 7, and David also recognized the importance of God's grace to His chosen ones. David sees the expressions of God's grace corporately and extols God's character by citing God's righteousness (v.6), compassion, longsuffering and love (v.8), grace (v.10), mercy (v.9 & 10), Fatherly care (v. 13), and faithfulness (v. 17).

David concludes the psalm with an admonition to the angels, hosts and all who serve the Lord and do His will to praise Him in light of the wonders he has recalled. He ends the psalm, as he began, with a reminder to his own soul to bless the Lord.

We have looked briefly at two examples of preaching the gospel to yourself from the Old Testament. In the New Testament both Paul and Peter were also painfully aware of the need for reminders as well. In Ephesians 2:11-12, Paul says this:

> Therefore **remember**, that formerly you, the Gentiles in the flesh, who are called "Uncircumcision" by the so-called "Circumcision," which is performed in the flesh by human hands--**remember** that you were at that time separate from Christ, excluded from the commonwealth of Israel, and strangers to the covenants of promise, having no hope and without God in the world. But now in Christ Jesus you who formerly were far off have been brought near by the blood of Christ.

Paul knows that many of the Ephesian believers were prone to memory lapses concerning their former life as licentious Gentiles. He exhorts them to remember the disadvantages inherent in that position. His desire is for them to recall that

THEY WERE:		THEY ARE:
Separate from Christ/ Far off		Brought Near/In Christ
Excluded from Israel	***BUT NOW***	Fellow citizens
Strangers to the Covenant of promise		Fellow partakers of the promise (3:6)
Without Hope/ Without God		Members of God's Household

Their former position represents their lives apart from God. They *were* positionally on the left side of the fork. Paul's desire is to bring this and their new position in Christ to the forefront of their thinking. He does so by contrasting their old position with their new one in Christ through the use of the phrase "but now." He emphasizes the change that has affected them individually and united them to the Body as a whole. As they are reminded of these truths, they are enabled to live out the Christian life as outlined in the last three chapters of Ephesians by Paul. It is only when they are mindful of who they are and from where they have come that they are appropriately empowered to walk in a manner worthy of the calling with which they have been called (Ephesians 4:1). Sustained right side living flows from a heart that abides in the truth in regards to its real identity.

The Apostle Peter provides a second example of the importance of reminding ourselves of what we already know. 2 Peter 1:9-15 says:

> For he who lacks these qualities is blind or short-sighted, having **forgotten** his purification from his former sins. Therefore, brethren, be all the more diligent to make certain about His calling and choosing you; for as long as you practice these things you will never stumble; for in this way the entrance into the eternal kingdom of our Lord and Savior Jesus Christ will be abundantly supplied to you. Therefore, I shall always be ready to **remind** you of these things, even though you already know them, and have been established in the truth which is present with you. And I consider it right, as long as I am in this earthly dwelling, to stir you up by way of **reminder**, knowing that the laying aside of my earthly dwelling is imminent, as also our Lord Jesus Christ has made clear to me. And I will also be diligent that at any time after my departure you may be able to **call these things to mind.**

Peter, just as Paul in the above Ephesians passage, reminds the saints to whom he is writing of their previous condition. He says that if they lack godly character it is because they have forgotten the "purification from their former sins." He sees it as his ministry to remind believers of who they are and of God's graciousness in calling and choosing them. He has a clear calling to live at the ready to remind them of the "things that they already know, that they have been established in and that are present in them." He recognizes that retention of this knowledge is the only means available to prevent stumbling (v.10). In saying this, Peter supplies the solution for permanent residence on the right side of the Fork.

Peter and Paul both demonstrate that preaching the gospel to ourselves includes reminders both of who we were and who we now are. This contrasting pattern is seen in several Scriptural passages which use the phrase "but God" or "but now."

- Romans 3:19-22 "Now we know that whatever the Law says, it speaks to those who are under the Law, that every mouth may be closed, and all the world may become accountable to God; because by the works of the Law no flesh will be justified in His sight; for through the Law comes the knowledge of sin. **But now** apart from the Law the righteousness of God has been manifested, being witnessed by the Law and the

Prophets, even the righteousness of God through faith in Jesus Christ for all those who believe...."

This passage reminds us that we were condemned under law, but now, as those positionally in Christ, we have a righteousness from God that is imparted apart from the Law.

- Romans 5:6-10 "For while we were still helpless, at the right time Christ died for the ungodly. For one will hardly die for a righteous man; though perhaps for the good man someone would dare even to die. **But God** demonstrates His own love toward us, in that while we were yet sinners, Christ died for us. Much more then, having now been justified by His blood, we shall be saved from the wrath of God through Him. For if while we were enemies, we were reconciled to God through the death of His Son, much more, having been reconciled we shall be saved by His life."

Here, just two chapters away from the previous example, we have Paul writing to the Roman church to explain that they were in the unenviable position of being enemies of God. Then he reminds them that God demonstrated His love toward us, while we were still sinners. He did not expect us to "clean up our acts" and make ourselves acceptable to Him before He saved us. He reconciles us and delivers us from His wrath through the blood of Christ. With incredible economy of words, Paul reminds the Romans of both aspects of their justification in a single verse (v.10). He says that they are both forgiven and declared righteous. They are reconciled to God through Jesus' death (forgiven), and, much more, they are saved through His life (Christ's righteously lived life is credited to them). The bleakness of the past is viewed through the distinctly different lens of the glorious present and future.

- 1 Corinthians 1:26-31 "For consider your calling, brethren, that there were not many wise according to the flesh, not many mighty, not many noble; **but God** has chosen the foolish things of the world to shame the wise, and God has chosen the weak things of the world to shame the things which are strong, and the base things of the world and the despised, God has chosen, the things that are not, that He might nullify the things that are, that no man should boast before God. ***But by His doing*** you are in Christ Jesus who became to us wisdom from God and righteousness and sanctification and redemption, that, just as it is written, 'Let him who boasts, boast in the Lord.'"

In this passage we are reminded that the gospel is for those who are weak and broken. Grace is not for the wise or the "things that are" but rather is extended to the needy at God's initiative.

- Ephesians 2:1-6 "And you were dead in your trespasses and sins, in which you formerly walked according to the course of this world, according to the prince of the power of the air, of the spirit that is now working in the sons of disobedience. Among them we too all formerly lived in the lusts of the flesh, indulging the desires of the flesh and of the mind, and were by nature children of wrath, even as the rest. ***But God***, being rich in mercy, because of His great love with which He loved us, even when we were dead in our transgressions, made us alive together with Christ (by grace you have been saved), and raised us up with Him, and seated us with Him in the heavenly places, in Christ Jesus."

Again Paul reminds of the dire former condition of the believer in contrast with the incredible blessing resulting from union with Christ. Preaching the gospel to ourselves is merely reminding ourselves that what God says is true of us.

Assuming we now have a better picture of what it means to "preach the gospel to ourselves," how can we know that we've really "heard" the message? Whenever our hearts really "hear" the message of the gospel, we feel schizophrenic. We experience emotions that seem to be conflicting. While our intellect tells us that being brought low and being lifted up are contradictory positions, in the gospel we recognize that they are not mutually exclusive sentiments. Each time we hear the gospel with our hearts, we are simultaneously brought down and lifted up. We are both humbled and exalted as we see the depth of our sin and love and value that He places on us through the magnitude of His grace. When we experience the grace of God, we feel good and bad at the same time. This is how we can know that we've been reminded of our identity. This is how we can be assured that we know the things that we know. The exposure of our sin is humbling. It is difficult to allow ourselves to fully acknowledge the desperation of our real condition. We are sinful through and through. To not only know this in our heads, but to understand or "hear" it with our hearts is painful, and we are broken when it grips us. Yet it is only from this position that we are able to receive the good news that grace is available for those who are broken. This is what lifts us up. To be reminded and to comprehend that He loves us and does not condemn us causes our spirits to soar. Whenever we move from left side living to right side identity in Christ we have been simultaneously humbled and honored.

And, finally, we need to recognize that what truly changes us is not merely a recitation of the truths of the gospel message, but rather change is wrought when our hearts are gripped by the immeasurable *cost* to God the Father and Son to make those truths reality for us. It is not enough for me to know that my sins are forgiven; I must be gripped with the fact that they are forgiven because Jesus became sin for me. Change will not be produced if I simply remember that I will one day wear a crown and be robed in glory; I must know that He forfeited His place of exaltation, surrendered His crown and left glory to come to a hostile, foreign place and live a perfect life and die an undeserved death for me. Mere acknowledgment of my spiritual healing will not be sufficient for transformation; I must see that I am healed because He was wounded. His hands are the ones that bear the scars, not mine. I must recognize that I do not receive punishment for my sin because Christ bore the punishment that I deserved while He was innocent. I am shielded and sheltered because He was exposed. I always have an audience before the Father because on the Cross, He was denied access to the Father's face. The lyrics to a contemporary praise chorus provide a wonderful example of recognizing that the cost of my forgiveness and acceptance is what captures our hearts and motivates us to praise and acts which honor our King.

Amazing Love
By: Billy Foote

I'm *forgiven*, because you were *forsaken*,
I'm *accepted*, you were *condemned*,
I'm *alive* and well, your Spirit is within me,
Because you *died* and rose again.

Amazing love, how can it be,
That you my King would die for me?
Amazing love, I know it's true,
It's my joy to honor you.
In all I do, I honor you.[6] (emphasis mine)

And it is not enough to know that He liberated me from slavery; I must be overwhelmed with the price at which my liberation was obtained.

As I write this, the United States is one week into the second Gulf War. There is continuous media coverage of events as they are unfolding in Iraq. A steady stream of politicians and top ranking military officials parade across our living room television screens. It is so easy for us as self-righteous Americans to look down in condemnation on Sadaam Hussein and his political régime. As we hear of the flagrant disregard of Geneva Convention guidelines for war and of the atrocities Sadaam Hussein and his regime leaders commit against their own people, we are so quick to conclude that we would never behave in such a reprehensible manner. As I watched the coverage, I was particularly struck by an interview conducted with an unnamed, low ranking member of the U.S. armed services. I believe the intent of the embedded media correspondent was to present the sentiments and condition of morale of the military "grass roots." This young man was asked to express his opinion of the enemy who had been repeatedly firing rounds of munitions toward his current location. As the camera zoomed in for a close up, the compassionate look in the soldier's eyes haunted me as his words pierced my heart. This is what he said: "The difference between me and an Iraqi soldier is that I am willing to come to his country, fight and die for his freedom, and he doesn't even know what freedom is all about." In that moment, I was struck by the realization that my Savior could have uttered these very words about me. While I self-righteously view myself as superior to the morality of the Iraqi soldiers and leaders, I am just like them. I am hostile to the very One whose only mission is to free me. Jesus was willing to come into hostile territory, willing to die for my liberation, when I did not even know what freedom was.

Even still, I am willing to live in bondage, under the influence of a lying dictator, even when he and his regime have already been defeated. I persist in resisting the One who came to rescue me, deliver me and liberate me. I am so prone to "left side living" on the Fork. Had the young serviceman voiced these words with an air of aggression or self-righteousness, they would not have had nearly the impact on my soul as they did. The obvious sympathy he felt for the Iraqi people, which mirrored the kindness of my Savior, was my undoing.

Two weeks after seeing the television interview of the young soldier I received an e-mail sent out to all Navigator staff members from Alan Andrews. Alan currently serves as the U.S. Director for The Navigators, an interdenominational Christian organization. In it he informed us that a staff family's son, serving as a pilot of an F-15E Strike Eagle plane, died while on a bombing mission in Northern Iraq. The 30 year old was described as a man who exemplified what faith in Christ, honor and duty, and a life of excellence meant. He leaves behind a grieving wife and parents. Yet we are assured that he is now at home with the Lord. He went to liberate the Iraqi people not only at the risk of his life, as was the case of the young serviceman interviewed on the television, but he went at the cost of his life. He provides an even clearer picture of the Savior in that Jesus did not come to set me free merely at the risk of His life, but He secured my freedom at the cost of His life. Recognizing the cost of my salvation is what melts me and transforms my life. It is what motivates me to abide on the "right side of the Fork." The gospel is not an idle word for us; indeed, it is our life. Because of our union with Christ through the gospel, we have everything that we need for life and godliness.

For those of us predisposed to visual learning, the Fork Illustration provides a framework for seeing the truth of the gospel message. May this visual representation aid us in remembering who we are and in living as beloved children who walk by the Spirit of God.

END NOTES

Chapter One – The Fork Illustration

1. C. J. Mahaney with Kevin Meath, *The Cross Centered Life* (Sisters, OR: Multnomah Publishers, Inc., 2002 by Sovereign Grace Ministries), page 25.
2. Edmund Clowney, *The Church* (Downers Grove, IL: InterVarsity Press, 1995), page 87.

Chapter Two – Seeing Scripture on the Fork

1. Jerry Bridges, *The Discipline of Grace* (Colorado Springs, CO: NavPress, 1994), page 24.
2. Paul Miller, *The Person of Jesus*, Leader's Manual (Telford, PA: seeJesus.net), page 212.
3. James Montgomery Boice, *Romans, Justification by Faith*, vol. 1, *Romans 1 – 4* (Grand Rapids, MI: Baker Book House, 1991), pages 375-376.
4. Boice, page 376.
5. Josiah Bancroft, *Sonship* (Oreland, PA: World Harvest Mission, 1997), pages 8-9 – 8-10.
6. The Works of Jonathan Edwards (Peabody, MA: Hendrickson Publishers, Inc., 2000), page 835.
7. Brennan Manning, *The Ragamuffin Gospel* (Sisters, OR: Multnomah Publisher, Inc., 1990), page 132.
8. Henry Nouwen, *The Return of the Prodigal Son* (New York, NY: Doubleday, 1992), page 36.
9. Reported by Timothy J. Keller in a message entitled "The Prodigal Son," given at Redeemer Presbyterian Church, New York, NY, January 11, 1998.
10. Henry Nouwen, *The Return of the Prodigal Son* (New York, NY: Doubleday, 1992), page 69.
11. Nouwen, page 78.
12. William Hendriksen and Simon J. Kistemaker, *New Testament Commentary, Colossians* (Grand Rapids, MI: Baker Books, 1964), page 16.
13. Hendriksen and Kistemaker, page 18.

156

14. Webster's New World Dictionary of the American Language, Second College Edition, World Publishing Company, 1970, David B. Guarlnik, Editor in Chief, New York and Cleveland, page 80.

Chapter Three – Practical Examples on the Fork

1. Reported by Timothy J. Keller in a message entitled "The Messengers of the Gospel," given at Redeemer Presbyterian Church, New York, NY, May 31, 1998.
2. C. S. Lewis, Mere Christianity (New York, NY: Macmillian Publishing Co., Inc., 1943), page 112.
3. Webster's New World Dictionary of the American Language, Second College Edition, World Publishing Company, 1970, David B. Guarlnik, Editor in Chief, New York and Cleveland, page 305.

Chapter 4 – The Holy Spirit on the Fork

1. J. I. Packer, Knowing God (Downers Grove, IL: InterVarsity Press, 1973), page 60.
2. J.R.R. Tolkien, The Fellowship of the Rings (New York, NY: Ballentine Books, 1954), p. 356-357.
3. J.I. Packer, Keep In Step with the Spirit (Grand Rapids, MI: Fleming H. Revell, 1984) page 66.
4. Herman Ridderbos, Paul: An Outlilne of His Theology, translated by John Richard DeWitt (Grand Rapids, MI: Eerdmans Publishing Company, 1966), page 65.
5. Steve McVey, Grace Walk (Eugene, OR: Harvest House Publishers, 1995), page 137.
6. Reported by Timothy J. Keller in a message entitled "Receiving the Fulllness – Part 3," given at Redeemer Presbyterian Church, New York, NY, September 13,1992.
7. Keller, September 13, 1992.
8. Reported by Paige Benton in a message entitled "Grace Saves Us," given at the Fruit of Grace Western Regional Conference, Denver Colorado, September 28, 2001.

9. Reported by Timothy J. Keller in a message entitled "Glory in Your Life," given at Redeemer Presbyterian Church, New York, NY, November 3, 2002.
10. Edmund Clowney, *The Church* (Downers Grove, IL: InterVarsity Press, 1995), page 47.

Chapter 5 – Misconceptions on the Fork

1. *Gospel Transformation*, Leader's Manual (Oreland, PA: World Harvest Mission, 2001), page 113.
2. Thomas Watson, *The Doctrine of Repentance* (Carlisle, PA: The Banner of Truth Trust, 1987; originally published 1668), page 18.
3. Thomas Watson, page 18.
4. Paul Miller, *Love Walked Among Us* (Colorado Springs, CO: NavPress, 2001), page 49.
5. Thomas Watson, *The Doctrine of Repentance* (Carlisle, PA: The Banner of Truth Trust, 1987; originally published 1668), page 18.
6. Thomas Watson, page 18.
7. Thomas Watson, page 39
8. *Webster's New World Dictionary of the American Language*, Second College Edition, World Publishing Company, 1970, David B. Guarlnik, Editor in Chief, New York and Cleveland, page1308.
9. Edward T. Welch, *When People Are Big and God is Small* (Phillipsburg, NJ: P & R Publishing, 1997), page 24.
10. Thomas Watson, *The Doctrine of Repentance* (Carlisle, PA: The Banner of Truth Trust, 1987; originally published 1668), page 18.
11. Thomas Watson, page 45.
12. Thomas Watson, page 18.
13. Rick Downs, *Sonship* (Oreland, PA: World Harvest Mission, 1997), page 7-12.
14. Paul Miller, *The Person of Jesus*, Leader's Manual (Telford, PA: seeJesus.net), page 231.

Chapter 6: The Enemies of the Believer on the Fork

1. Elyse Fitzpatrick, *Idols of the Heart* (Phillipsburg, NJ: P & R Publishing, 2001), pages 198 -199.
2. Edmund Clowney, *The Church* (Downers Grove, IL: InterVarsity Press, 1995), page 172.
3. *Gospel Transformation*, Leader's Manual (Oreland, PA: World Harvest Mission, 2001), page 76.
4. *Gospel Transformation*, Leader's Manual (Oreland, PA: World Harvest Mission, 2001), page 77.
5. Edward T. Welch, *Addictions – A Banquet in the Grave* Phillipsburg, NJ: P & R Publishing, 2001), page 157.
6. Elyse Fitzpatrick, Idols of the Heart (Phillipsburg, NJ: P & R Publishing, 2001), page 158.
7. Reported by Timothy J. Keller in a message entitled "Self Control – Part 3," given at Redeemer Presbyterian Church, New York, NY, April 22, 1990.
8. David Powlison, X-Ray Questions: Drawing Out the Whys and Wherefores of Human Behavior (Glenside, PA: Christian Counseling and Educational Foundation, 1999), The Journal of Biblical Counseling 18(1), pages 2-9.
9. Elyse Fitzpatrick, Idols of the Heart (Phillipsburg, NJ: P & R Publishing, 2001), page 158.

Chapter 7: The Body on the Fork Illustration

1. Edmund Clowney, *The Church* (Downers Grove, IL: InterVarsity Press, 1995), page 163.
2. Douglas Kelly, Systematic Theology II, Ecclesiology & Sacraments, Syllabus & Notes, ST516, (Jackson, MS: Reformed Theological Seminary, Winter 2002), page 1.
3. *Webster's New World Dictionary of the American Language*, Second College Edition, World Publishing Company, 1970, David B. Guarlnik, Editor in Chief, New York and Cleveland, page 288.
4. Edmund Clowney, *The Church* (Downers Grove, IL: InterVarsity Press, 1995), page 16.

5. Reported by Timothy J. Keller in a message entitled "People of God," given at Redeemer Presbyterian Church, New York, NY, February 13, 1994.

6. http://ourworld.compuserve.com/homepages/beit avanim_chaiot, 04/01/03.

7. Reported by Joseph Stowell in a message entitled "Stuck on Me," given at The Cove, Asheville, NC, November 5, 1993.

8. Edmund Clowney, *The Church* (Downers Grove, IL: InterVarsity Press, 1995), page 30.

9. William Hendriksen and Simon J. Kistemaker, *New Testament Commentary, Colossians* (Grand Rapids, MI: Baker Books, 1964), page 129.

10. Edmund Clowney, *The Church* (Downers Grove, IL: InterVarsity Press, 1995), page 199.

11. Edmund Clowney, page 103.

12. Edmund Clowney, page 98.

13. Edmund Clowney, page 69.

14. Edmund Clowney, page 64.

15. Edmund Clowney, page 240.

16. Edmund Clowney, page 103.

17. Douglas Kelly, Systematic Theology II, Ecclesiology & Sacraments, Syllabus & Notes, ST516, (Jackson, MS: Reformed Theological Seminary, Winter 2002), page 34.

18. Douglas Kelly, page 36-37.

19. Edmund Clowney, *The Church* (Downers Grove, IL: InterVarsity Press, 1995), page 104.

Chapter 8: Speaking to Yourself with "Fork" Tongue

1. Jerry Bridges, *The Discipline of Grace* (Colorado Springs, CO: NavPress, 1994), page 8.

2. R. Laird Harris, Gleason L. Archer, Jr. and Bruce K. Waltke, *Theological Wordbook of the Old Testament* (Chicago, IL: Moody Press, 1980), page 922.

3. Peter C. Craigie, *The New International Commentary on the Old Testament*, Deuteronomy (Grand Rapids, MI: Eerdmans Publishing Company, 1976), page 372.

4. Peter C. Craigie, page 372.
5. James Montgomery Boice, *Psalms* (Grand Rapids MI: Baker Books, XXXX), page 834.
6. Used by permission CCLI # 237085.

ISBN 1-41204456-1